AuthorHouse™ UK
1663 Liberty Drive
Bloomington, IN 47403 USA
www.authorhouse.co.uk
Phone: 0800.197.4150

Published by AuthorHouse 12/05/2018

ISBN: 978-1-7283-8086-5 (sc)
978-1-7283-8042-1 (e)

Print information available on the last page.

This book is printed on acid-free paper.

authorHOUSE®

THE WAY OF THE INTERNAL GATE

LIVING PRINCIPLES

ADE FINCH

Dedication

This book is dedicated to the one true love of my life Alicia.

Finding my wife confirmed to me, that what seemed the impossible could be achieved with commitment, patience and keeping the faith. Her continued support and loving heart are the reason this book is now in your hand.

Table of Contents

Acknowledgements

I wish to extend a heartfelt thank you to the following people who were imperative in the creation of this publication; my wife Alicia, for her encouragement and input. The practitioners of The Way of the Internal Gate; Gavin, Janette, Phil, Jennifer and Darren who made working on this publication so much fun, as we always have when we train. To my friend behind the lens Doug, who provided the photography to express The Way of the Internal Gate in pictures. This revision would not be nearly as polished if it were not for my friend Ian, editors and publisher who provided a great service and advice.

Living Principles

The intention behind this book is to provide you with an overview and universal perspective on the key core 'living principles' that will act as a catalyst to enhance your martial art prowess. This is the practice of The Way of the Internal Gate martial art, or IG for short. My hope is that exposure to this art will introduce you to its unique approach and expression. This will focus and concentrate on the enrichment of your self-understanding to cultivate the heart of the martial artist, where not only do you benefit but humanity as a whole.

By its own nature, IG is a quick and succinct approach to self-preservation. Therefore, you may find that there are short paragraphs in some of the content. However, I urge you to return and reread the material often. As your own awareness and martial art prowess improves, you will gain further insight and benefit from these passages.

I am optimistic and hopeful that a wide range of experienced individuals will be willing to read this material, from the beginner or novice to the expert or master. With this wide audience in mind, I have started with a foundation of IG's perspective, which moves on to the principles of one's journey along the way and application to training with a feeling of continuous growth.

So, here are my personal thoughts and feelings on my philosophy of the totality of martial arts: The Way of the Internal Gate. I hope you enjoy this material and gain great benefit, as I believe this book to be paramount to anyone beginning their martial art voyage and for those already on their way. This material could provide the necessary ingredients to fill in the blanks to your own questions in martial arts and complement your personal voyage of evolution. Either way, this book has been written for you not only to show some of my own personal realisation, but to help you discover some of your own.

Regardless of your martial arts background or current training, IG is not just for the individual who wants another method or path to train. It is based on the principles of the human being and not bound by any other restrictions. As such, it can help you improve and upgrade your martial art prowess and self-understanding whether or not training has already been undertaken.

So, to make my intentions clear, this book and future volumes are for the individual who chooses martial arts for its practical life-saving applications and life improvement, with an idea eventually to harness and encourage an altruistic step up in humanity. The Way of the Internal Gate Martial Arts' sole aim and mission is ultimately to elevate, enhance and upgrade the human being to a higher level of expression and self-awareness, and achieving this through the ascension of martial arts prowess.

Ade Finch
Founder of The Way of the Internal Gate

Short Biography of The Way of the Internal Gate

The Way of the Internal Gate originated from a vast amount of research into the possibilities of the human being at all levels in an attempt to get to the root of what martial arts truly meant to me.

Although I began my martial arts training in the traditional methods of Japanese Jujutsu, Karate and Bujutsu weaponry, Korean Taekwondo, Chinese boxing, Muay Thai from Thailand and many of the arts that involved striking, locking and grappling natures, I would spend time considering a great variety of methods comparing with other martial artists and discovering all that I could to further my knowledge.

I enjoyed cross-training with anyone who practised any martial art and those that I had studied to understand if there were any differences, which more often than not there were. I was on a quest to find all that was possible with my own means; I was drawn in with intensity into the world of martial arts and what it involved, how it was used and its place in the world. Questions arose throughout my training: What was this fascination inside of me? Why did it mean so much? And many more to help me explore my mental approach. These questions became quintessential to my personal growth, not only as a martial artist but as a human being.

I always sensed a feeling whilst training that I could not express in words. From the beginning of my martial arts journey, there was a gradual welling up inside of me that led to such a diverse curriculum of training and an obsession with martial arts. I questioned all I did and why, such as why am I learning a particular method of martial arts right now? I didn't realise this straight away, but eventually after years of self-reflection I came to understand that I was after the reason and root of what martial arts meant to me. Why did I learn to defend myself in more than one art? Why was I learning to hurt another human in different ways? How did these questions impact me on a psychological level?

My questions became deeper or harder to find the answers as I grew from one art to another. What hid in the background of these intentions? I cannot say exactly when it happened. I was training every day and seeking out what others thought or felt about it to gain some kind of perspective. However, I started to doubt myself and all the training I had practised and researched. I asked all those who I studied under and tried to question whoever was most senior in those organisations, but I never found my own answers. The option to live in another country to train with the head teachers was not viable due to finances.

For whatever reason I needed time to understand this feeling, so I stopped all formal training within any tradition. I elected to train by myself without the use of official resources or help from others so that I could find this elusive and burning desire that I felt within.

I had many questions I wanted to answer, and I understood that time was needed to do so. Beginning with the simple articulation of my body in executing a punch, a kick and types of throws and so on, I looked into the detail of simple movement. These became the foundational steps to a philosophy as rich and deep to warrant writing volumes and volumes of tireless enquiries – which you will become aware of by reading this book. These were the building blocks to a refinement of those years of constant practice and searching.

This resulted in a unique realisation along the way that helped greatly in the direction of my training. Eventually, this led to opening a club on 1 April 2004. The purpose now was twofold: Firstly, to test my own ability and see if I could cope with a class. I'd had a few one-to-one tuitions by this point but now needed to challenge myself further. Secondly, to provide another way of training in martial arts that empowers the individual to follow their own heart and unearth a journey of self-discovery. A martial art that involves a unique, holistic and realistic approach which continues to evolve. This club eventually became The Way of the Internal Gate.

My training aims to provide close personal guidance in smaller groups and seminars all over the world. The Way of the Internal Gate is not a product of previous martial arts; it is the awareness and realisations of the human being. In fact, it is a cessation of organised methods and respect for the laws of nature and humanity. Interestingly, it was not until I detached myself from previous formal training that things started to click for me. This could be a unique position for me, or possibly this could happen to you. Only exposure to IG will give you the answer. Thus, IG is the vehicle for the individual to find and express oneself with their true ability in martial arts.

The Way of the Internal Gate is a method to explore if you are or want to take the martial arts path as your way in life, understanding that not all answers reside outside of your own mind. A unique soul who realises the gift resides within; self-understanding is the solution to martial arts prowess whether you train in groups or alone.

CHAPTER 1

Root of a Martial Artist

'The Way of the Internal Gate is the ascension and evolution of the human being through its unique and individual application of martial arts.'

Ade Finch
Founder of The Way of the Internal Gate

In this opening chapter, our journey looks at the essence, the core and what can be considered as the root for true growth of the martial artist from the perspective of IG. Their intentions create a marvellous attitude towards training and life. This induces the thoughts to manifest a more beneficial climate for cultivation and, where necessary, change.

Now, let us dive into the living principles, the philosophy upon which all IG training firmly stands. These are supported by firm bedrock tenets that help to evolve the human in martial endeavours and lead to altruistic actions. Let us begin with the chief elements upon which all training takes its position to move forwards on the path of evolution.

The Journey Is Individual

The first principle to understand is that each one of us must travel our martial art voyage alone for the most part, in the psychological sense. This is not meant as a discouragement. In fact, the reason for this is to take responsibility for that which we need to grow. When I say alone I'm referring to when training and learning, as this affects each of us differently and shows something that is relevant only to you.

I believe that if you emphasise this idea in your training, it will help you to learn, grow and absorb martial arts much faster. Also, it is better because there will be no contest between individuals. All too often, the competitive nature of humanity is responsible for holding us back from our true course. We allow this to happen, rather than adhere to a degree of suffering, for a more righteous mode of life. It is easier to place our intention and focus on what is in front of us, and face the challenges of another for something such as accolades, trophies or respect. However, to face your inner opponent and overcome a mental block or psychological change is difficult, even painful. It will not be the same as reaching a goal, should this be overcome, but it will have a fundamental change in your outlook on life.

The contest between humans can, unfortunately, breed negativity and be counterproductive. There is also a healthy way of a contest, which requires balance and understanding as the key to unlocking its potential.

This is a mature way of training as it emphasises individual growth and the true path to self-discovery through martial arts training. As your attention begins to turn inwards, the noises and distractions that can affect us from outside are gradually reduced. This increases your ability by cultivating a more stable mind as part of your foundation. You must not worry about others; rather, focus on your development as we share with others. We gain genuine experiences through learning with each other, and understanding our training resonates differently within each of us. Being responsible and looking at ourselves are the important and key messages here.

Experience in Sharing

I have a motto to describe the essence of IG's existence and my own approach to martial arts training that can be transferred to all other areas in your life: 'Independent enquiry with interdependent discovery is the key to self-mastery'. Even though each of our martial arts voyage is unique, we grow tremendously from sharing in each other's experience. Clearly, another person will rarely be going through the exact experience of training as you, but they may have been through something similar.

What is individual is the impact it can have on each of us. Someone may experience a fear they need to overcome, whereas another may gain insight and faith in oneself from the same encounter. Regardless of this, martial arts rely on the human aspects of being social; therefore, we need to understand humanity. Simply put, you could train for a decade and still be conquered by a novice. If you have not experienced what happens during human conflict, then you cannot consider the myriad of bizarre responses humanity holds in its hands.

If you train by yourself with no other human contact, you will not expose yourself to the unusual behaviour of how humans react to your training. Those responses can change during human conflict. Many times when you see a competition between two known styles of martial arts, under duress, core principles are quite often thrown out of the window and a slugging match ensues. Understanding the human aspect and reality makes sense to me because those core principles adhered to might not work in every situation. The only true way is to test your capabilities under a degree of healthy pressure.

In addition to this, there are the altruistic and social principles to consider once a better level of understanding has occurred.

So, once you have begun to test your ability to attain a good degree of competence, to achieve a good practical use, you must take social behaviour into your training. Let us look at a simple strike like a punch from a specific stance. Once you have established and validated that this technique is useful and strong, you will want to test it in social circumstances. This will change how the method is executed. I will be expanding more on this in the next volume of the series. In an altruistic circumstance, you may only wish to subdue and control your attacker without hurting them because they may be under the influence or not themselves.

The other part of altruism relates to your methods revealing an insight into your core being. For example, recognising a fault or negative behaviour, and taking remedial steps to alter this part of your conscience. This would be beneficial for the greater good of your life, which in turn improves the situation for those you are in contact with.

These first two living principles set the tone as you embark on your adventure into the realms of martial arts; it is vital that they are understood independently and interdependently. Applied with the knowledge of their benefit to you in your training, they become a fulcrum to leverage your own understanding. They create a focal point of reassurance; you are heading in a better direction for cultivation and overall improvement. The results will speak for themselves.

Looking as a Whole

I have found that we need to look at our whole being to grow as a complete human and martial artist. The full spectrum of Homo sapiens is to be experienced, cultivated, explored and trained. We gain insight from training with each other, learning about ourselves, and using each other as mirrors to see our strengths and weaknesses – but there must be no limiting aspects. In other words, we train in our entirety to gain a greater insight into our true being. We gain this insight by looking at our past, present and future.

The more we explore our full capabilities, the more advantage we can have over our opponents and entry into our own wisdom. Beware, as the adversary is not necessarily in front of you! This is one of the defining principles of IG: the inner opponent, which I touched on before. The mindset is more important than the accumulation of knowledge. By looking inwards at your own fears, doubts and the thoughts that hold you back, you must keep the inner opponent in mind because you can be taken down a different path.

Through Self-Defence to Self-Discovery

'Through self-defence to self-discovery' is another philosophical motto I use to convey the meaning of martial arts at its base level. When you first begin training for non-sport orientated martial arts, the two main aspects of cultivation should be in learning to defend one's life whilst nurturing this in tandem with discovering more of yourself in the process. In fact, one of the greatest realisations that steered me in my own development was the birth of this knowledge through self-discovery. You can enhance your chances of defending yourself. This won't apply, if you choose to practice martial arts for reasons such as fitness. Again, as I've previously stated, IG training looks at preserving life and self-realisations through what at first appear as mere self-protecting methods.

I started my training club using 'Through Self-Defence to Self-Discovery' as its name, as I knew I would be teaching all kinds of people with different feelings and experiences. So, in this early phase, I emphasised that this is martial arts. I believe this maxim sums up the baby steps of the focus and training in the realm of martial arts. Much like a caterpillar that metamorphosizes from a cocoon, opening its eyes for the first time as a butterfly. It is this feeling that you strive for as a martial artist. It is a hint in the way of training. What do you think?

Ultimate Meaning

As my own training unveiled before me, it became clear that the emphasis of martial skill and using it as a medium to find myself was all that were necessary in training. My own realisations came from testing my ideas with those of others and the approaches used in traditional and non-traditional martial arts. I guess I have always wanted to believe in myself, and I had to do that in the one thing I truly loved. There are endless ways to train and each individual has their motivations to do so, which can alter throughout the course of their existence. However, for me, the ultimate meaning became a towering lighthouse shining to reveal a ropey path down upon a sea of what seemed endless eventualities, with no certainty of accomplishments other than to follow the light and experience the unknown instinct. This has always been my way: to find the truth in training and the human being. Now I train in these truths and have penned some of them here for you, in case these words strike a chord that the unknown allows you to glimpse and follow with your own heart. This is the message of IG. It cannot be found without relinquishing a measure of control to allow your instincts and senses to pierce through your reality.

Despite the truth that you can use martial arts experience to improve your physical ability, coordination, health, clarity of mind, confidence, strength and more, the ultimate meaning for me is to preserve one's life and become self-realised. These two elements will circle each other and create a vortex, blurring the distinction between them and forming a path – your own way. Think about where you are today in your training. What does it mean to you? Bear in mind that as I have trained, my own reasons have changed according to my circumstances. Yet, despite many, I have trained because there have always been the two golden truths in self-preservation and self-discovery at the very root of it all. It just took me many years to figure this out. Although, it was not only on an intellectual level as it is not possible to find using pure logic or intelligence. Your feelings must play an integral part; your instincts and whole being must be brought into play to discover all that is humanly possible. Only through immersing your entirety will you discover the ultimate meaning.

Spirit of Endurance

This living principle is a must for the serious martial artist. Endurance requires a kind of patience with yourself that forges the human on at times of spectacular hardship. This tenet acts like a shield from all the knockdowns, enabling you to get back up and go again and again. Just like the baby who is solely intent and determined to get that toy the adult keeps out of reach. No matter the number of knockdowns received, the determined and barely conditioned infant keeps going. They cry if they feel it is fruitless, and then simply move on to something else. How natural!

It is important to realise that genuine cultivation in training cannot be achieved immediately. As time goes by and your endurance builds, you expose yourself to your downfalls, doubts, fears and weaknesses. Then something begins to grow: self-belief – the first step in martial arts training. Maybe you will ask yourself if this can be done or if it is possible. When I first thought of opening a training club, I contemplated the name 'The Art of Self-Belief' because I was aware of the necessity for this. Martial arts are not a cult; however, it is if you choose a lifelong study that will continue to surprise and reward you forever. As long as you are prepared to put in the effort required for your own development, you will always succeed. In simple terms, the longer you invest in your growth, the more you will gain from it.

One of the underlying principles learnt through martial arts is the spirit of endurance. Keep the faith.

Spirit of Learning

Something all those I train in IG have cultivated is the spirit of learning. By now you may have sensed a pattern as one principle naturally leads into another. IG captures the essence and allows it to unfold without a tight grip on the conscious mind. As training is natural and so are we, this is the natural way. From enduring, from the exposure, you begin to open up and see things: How you respond under certain pressures. Why some people respond in particular ways to specific stimuli. Understanding what you enjoy from exercises that can bring out the best in you. The list goes on and on as you uncover layers of your mind through perception and realise your physical strengths and vulnerabilities. You begin to sense all these from new angles and with more appetite.

When you discover a part of how you see the world that can be misinterpreted, and you finally glimpse an insight into seeing the world with different eyes, this breathes excitement into your training and a new thirst to continue. This develops a fresh look from a more receptive mind, which helps to discover more about you and explores your inner world. This can only be carried out with a spirit of learning. It is important to understand the feeling this brings and to fully grasp the impact it can have on you. There is only one way to experience this – to train with this feeling and intention.

In your drive for perfection of martial arts prowess, you question yourself and the ways to attain that which you seek. Learning is cultivated – not academically, but with feeling and your whole being. In this mode, smartness succumbs to creativity. For example, I do not see myself as a teacher in the common sense because, to me, I am a learner. Those who train with me are my martial art friends. I help guide those who come to train with me because they see something in what I do that can benefit them. They respect me and the knowledge I have; however, it is the delivery of the training and the respect for the living principles that allow this mode to occur.

There is no difference under the stars; we are all human with equal possibilities and a need to unleash this somehow. Once acquired and the spirit of learning is fully embodied, bound by nothing the individual and their enthusiasm emanates from them. The spirit of learning creates a passion for something, and this passion is what gives life to anything. This is essential for everyone and benefits all humankind.

Cultivate a Flexible Mind

As you expose yourself to training, provided it is focused on your cultivation in every aspect, you will begin to nurture a flexible mind. The true essence of a flexible mind in training is the cornerstone of self-realisation. You cannot look internally to make a positive change without having the flexibility to adapt to new ideas. It is the same as looking in the mirror to confirm your look or make alterations such as changing your hair, clothes and appearance to suit the circumstance. The difference here is that you are perceiving how you think and feel and trying to find how best to alter these to suit your desired outcome, such as improving a technique or developing a strategy to work with different opponents and environments.

A flexible mind can be difficult to acquire, elusive and needs balance, which in itself requires a great amount of time and determination in your own training. The flexible mind is a martial artist's ally that allows you to open up and brave your own being whilst learning. You see, the real opponent lays dormant, deep within under many disguises, tricking and fooling its enemy, which is truth. The light of truth's quality shines bright. Yet, the inner opponent has become masterful in its trickery, deceit and lies. Much of this is due to defence mechanisms your ego has developed through life experiences. The mind can be fragile, so to look at yourself with complete honesty and discover where you need to improve or admit where you are not good can trigger a defence such as your inner opponent tricking you or deceiving your thoughts. It can display a portrayed version of a conditioned nature or learnt defence, but your true self is hidden. Can you remember as a child when you ran in the playground, recreation ground or through a field and never wanting the feeling to end because you are just being happy to run freely with little or no care? Over time, and in almost all cases because of time constraints in life, we lose this way of feeling. Until perhaps one day when you attend a seminar or retreat or something that reminds you of this feeling again. With the right spirit and with a flexible mind, there is hope to find your natural self through the correct training and mindset. This will lead to finding your true self.

What is implied here is that we all act naturally but to different degrees; in some way we have all been conditioned however it is viewed. IG training allows you to become acutely aware of this in your day-to-day life and provides the tools to either use this in your favour or confront the conditioned self to improve your quality of life. The latter is clearly an ultimate goal; however, you may be required to manipulate certain tendencies before you have the strength to make a positive improvement through a clearer understanding and expression of your own truth. Tendencies like a common response in a daily situation that has become so natural to you, or you might find you react in a very specific way under similar types of duress and attacks in your training.

To peel away the conditioned self, like the layers of an onion to reach a deeper level of naturalness and consciousness, you will be required to what may seem like going against your natural instinct. A physical example could be if you are attacked on your left side with a stick or hammer. Your natural response may be to raise your hands to defend your head. This might be natural, but, depending on the intent of the attacker, you could suffer further damage if the rest of your body freezes. If attacked in the same vein from the right side, you may always move in a certain direction and so on. In a social situation, you may find that specific comments or actions trigger a conditioned response that can have a negative or possibly a positive effect. Changing the response could alter the negative impact and protect you. Recognising the positive can give you an insight into human behaviour. This might sound odd to read because it is something you experience, but recognising these 'natural' tendencies is your path to self-discovery and The Way of the Internal Gate method to uncover your true self.

Either way, you will be gaining control over yourself in one aspect or another, thus gaining a feeling of growth and step in what will feel as a positive direction.

Honesty in Oneself

To gain insight into your true self, to even glimpse the truth of your genuine nature, you will need to have complete honesty with yourself. This is a difficult trait to acquire. Some find this easier than others. Either way, your own truthfulness often comes at a painful cost. However, do not dismay; here is where courage is mustered and faith in your true self is born. We all have skeletons in our closets and conditionings that prohibit our souls from shining. Remember that this honesty will reveal your path and help to excel your martial arts prowess.

By harmonising with your honesty and allowing it to shine, you will see your path as well as others before you. Listening to your honesty allows you to become aware of your weaknesses – from which you gain your real strengths and route to self-mastery.

Only Better or Worse

In my personal training and through its development, I came to realise that there is no right or wrong way as an absolute. There are actions, and they have a consequence. We as humans have a moral judgement. For example, as children many of us knew when we should not be doing something or pushed the boundaries of what is socially acceptable. More often than not we have a good moral compass, but to say philosophically 'that is right' or 'this is wrong' is more an idealism or belief in the mind of how we should conduct ourselves in society. In circumstances where you are learning a particular trade or method of how to build something, there are instructions and specific methods that often change because of social growth over time.

We can see that the safety and hazard precautions brought in from the late 20th century have altered how entire industries operate. We use the terms 'you're right' or 'that's right' as linguistic expressions, but performing an action and saying it is wrong or right can be down to interpretation whilst appreciating the circumstances.

In martial arts, to say that this is the right or wrong way to perform a movement can be dangerous because under unusual circumstances what seems right could put you in further danger. With facts, so easy to blur, the truth is often neglected and humanity can twist information rather than see it for what it is. This is often due to understanding the consequence of a situation, or a tinge of paranoia. A person can be performing an act of decency, yet this can be misconstrued if you believe it to be the opposite and it is taking advantage of someone. In such a situation, you will be playing out a negative scenario and making a judgement in that moment on a reasonable course of action.

In all instances, the human psyche is responsible because our senses feed the mind with information from the world around us, which the psyche, our mind, interprets. The information is raw, so to speak, but the parts of our psyche that are conditioned can look at something and interpret the meaning differently from the original intention. There are many occasions where two or more humans have been asked to look at the same picture or situation only to come away with two or more completely different views of that information. Being aware of this by giving it life to your training will open the path to creativity, along with other realisations. A measure will be born to test what you have learnt and questions to explore this subject further will follow on your path into martial arts.

This idea of no right or wrong bled into IG as I was discovering it, and I believe this has become a natural theme in the training now. I also believe that it is one of the truths of martial arts and a principle that can be used by anyone who wishes to improve themselves, whether in training or not. A truer perception of being right or wrong is the realisation of a better or worse way of doing something. For example, on a base level, you can do a simple punch. Now, there is no right or wrong way to punch; a punch is a label and term that is given to anyone using their arms to hit with their fist. We can look at this movement and say that there is no specific prescribed manner to punch. After 10 years or more training it is still a punch you are performing, and possibly doing better. The improvement comes from letting go of the boundaries and realising the truth given that each circumstance, one way to punch, may well be better than another. Allow this perception to linger in your mind as you read further.

Once I became aware of this simple realisation, this theory, I started to test it in all the things I did and do now. It has become the measure, and I continue to measure against this principle. To this day, it has become a central principle and core theme within IG training. I found this to be positive and more encouraging to my training colleagues because they now feel they have less inhibition and less concern or idealisms. They may scorn themselves in the moment if they feel they have not done something to the best of their abilities, but at the end of the day they don't say, 'Oh, that was not the right way of doing it!' Instead, they ask themselves how they could do it better. In training, do not put yourself down if you cannot do something just right or straight away. This is a waste of your energy. It is much better to allow your creativity to flow, to solve what might be called a problem and come up with a solution, or create a better way of expression.

IG training is innate to humanity; it is instinctive. This principle clearly shows how one learns to become more in tune with their inner voice. The mind becomes positive when channelled in this way. IG helps the individual channel their energy in whichever way helps them to become better. This can also be applied to one's own core or moral judgements. What is better or worse become your questions of measure. Clearly, it is worse if someone's actions have a negative impact or they do not seek to make it better instead of doing something with an altruistic and more beneficial impact on humankind. So, IG encourages making things better and becoming a better person. The essence of martial arts is – enhancing oneself and becoming a better human to improve life for other people. This is the altruistic nature of martial arts. This is IG.

Express Freely, Express Sincerely

Training gifts us all with the perfect opportunity in allowing us to be ourselves without restriction. To let us simply be. To apply this principle of expressing with freedom and sincerity means you must be prepared to let go of things that would impede or hold you back. This allows you to become closer to your instincts and be more natural. This is a positive attitude because when you step into your training class, backyard or wherever you go, you begin with the mindset of 'Well, it is difficult, but I want to be able to express myself in a free manner without any kind of restriction'. Also, to express yourself sincerely means that you are prepared to be and do something as honestly as you feel in that moment. You find yourself in a place where you express yourself in the moment and by the moment. If you feel embarrassed or held back in some way, as we can do at times in society, then your training can become a place where you allow your whole self to relax, be comfortable with who you are and release the shackles of the world and go for it.

In IG, it is paramount that people who I train let themselves go and find out who they are. They then begin to instinctively find out about themselves with me by their side in support, knowing that this is the foundation and the way to self-discovery. In IG, the inner voice echoes louder through the senses. By becoming aware of this, you will start to appreciate and get closer to a more honest expression of yourself in the moment and, as I have mentioned, by the moment. With this freedom, insight from within grows and you become better at sensing what holds you back, restricting you of self-expression and knowledge in all circumstances generally, which all points to upgrading oneself and your own abilities.

In your day-to-day life, this is not restricted to the upgrade of materials or your role at work; it is the totality of your life. IG is about the full spectrum of a human being's capabilities and capacity. It takes time and training to embrace this kind of feeling that allows you to come out with this expression. But the more you do it and the more honest you are with yourself, the more you feel you are improving and you feel the benefit of IG. It develops into a feeling of well-being and warmth that you begin to carry deep within you. It is impossible to put this actual feeling into words, but what a truly wonderful feeling to embrace.

Core Stability: Part 1 - Physical Exploration

To access your own potential and free the binds of your own conditionings, to do what is possible for you and explore yourself, you need to discover all your opportunities and total physical freedom. It is imperative to use exercises that gain access to your hidden potential, finding what is possible for you and bring about your own realisations.

Using other schools of thought, methods and ideas that emphasise aspects of martial arts training include wrestling, grappling or striking, avoidance, conditioning, clinching, tension or releasing force, or flowing exchanges, for example. It maybe something that is related to martial arts but not directly strength training, or stretching or breathing exercises. It could involve possible mental aspects, social behaviour or psychological understanding. This list is not exhaustive and there are literally hundreds if not thousands of methods you could try to achieve with many different attributes. But remember what you choose is down to your individual approach and self-awareness at that moment in your life or training, and it will change as you develop.

These ideas are great as an impetus to explore and understand yourself further, but take caution as you do not need to adhere to them so loyally that you don't listen to your own feelings and thoughts. Respect is distributed in a balanced manner to yourself as well as those who give you their time on your journey, whoever that may be and however it occurs.

It is truly a great achievement if you have found a way of training that suits you, and you're fully satisfied with what you do and it provides the gains you want, as humans can change over time. If this is the absolute case, you don't need to read any further because you have found what will unlock your own potential. However, if you are certain there is more to uncover and you are prepared to persist, please read on and you will access new regions of yourself. Also, it means that you are prepared to truly explore other ideas and be open-minded to other thought processes. This suggests you feel deep inside that your expression (your understanding of it) is connected to your internal needs, such as finding out how you respond under levels of stress and conflict, how to improve your capabilities, who you are and what does it mean to live a fulfilling life. These questions which all lead to self-discovery.

Curiosity is born from an internal need, and in this instance it could indicate that you have realised there is more to discover at your core. In this way, you convey the idea that you still believe there are more things to be found within you, there are more ideas and concepts to your own being, and you will find yourself in a position to discover and express them.

You will look at other ideas, remain open-minded and believe that one way is not necessarily the only answer. There may be other avenues to explore when you have a keen aptitude for uncovering all that you can. Again, if you feel that this is accurate in a single approach of training, then that is impressive. The reason you train also has a grip on your fulfilment of what you gain.

However, IG is an art based on exposure. Depending on where you are on your martial art journey, here exposure means having the faith in yourself to look at all the things that contact you. Exposing oneself to many avenues to gain as much insight into oneself does not necessarily mean doing as many arts as possible, but it does require openness to other thoughts, even from oneself.

Now, this is the idea of core stability and it requires you to ask yourself how to create core stability in your physique and physiology that will allow you to further your exploration. Because, you see, IG is quintessentially creating an impetus, a catalyst, so the actual exercises are not an end in themselves. They have been cultivated, conceived and created with the sole purpose to explore your true self and go beyond what you can see in your mind.

So, for example, core stability in our physiology means exercises will now be used and introduced as part of IG to help you explore your innermost being and discover ideas you may or may not have realised. The following example will help explain this. With these ideas, you will further your self-discovery. IG gives you the essential tools to take you to your next level.

The foundational step is to assist you in becoming aware of what you could develop. This can also expose what you do not need to develop so you can refine what is necessary for you and achieve what you have discovered. Let me try to break this down with a basic example, but please be aware that this is not a template for self-discovery.

Let us say that through one of the exercises in IG you discover that you leave an area of your body exposed for an easy counterstrike from your adversary after a movement such as a strike. At first, this is a simple movement you do without thought and are therefore unaware of this exposure. The foundational step is that you have now become aware of this. Your initial part of the movement may not need further refinement as you could have a strong and effective technique. However, you now know that something unique to you in the way you move is required for development in your overall goal. In this instance, the goal would be a non-telegraphed strike with a swift recovery of movement to reduce your exposure for a counter-attack. What you realise is a simple movement to reduce your exposure is needed to be developed.

Now you can see how difficult it is to explain IG in words. I have tried my best to describe this as clearly and pertinently as possible. However, when you get to the root of all things, words become difficult to explain a true expression. It is truly an experience. These are the living principles of IG that continue to evolve, upgrade and enhance the human being as well as the whole life of the human who trains in it.

CHAPTER 2

Martial Arts Prowess

'What was I going to get out of this martial art? So far, I have self-confidence in my ability and belief in my own inner strength.'

2nd Gate IG Exponent

We now turn to the expression of your physical abilities. Using the living principles in the first chapter, we explored how to enhance and upgrade your martial arts prowess, and how the IG exponent looks to cultivate creativity and reach physical potential and understanding. We now take a closer look at the foundation of IG's approach to martial art application and the building blocks to martial art talent. Through the exploration of the senses, a catalyst of ability is created with the formation of a martial arts journey.

Beginning the Path

Once the principles of the first chapter have begun to infuse into your training, the foundations to martial arts proficiency and understanding will appear as you undergo a biological alteration that befits your own natural propensities.

It takes time, patience and determination to cultivate, so it is imperative to accept that you have embarked on your own voyage of self-discovery regardless of what your purpose or original thoughts were. Personally, I feel this to be something rare and incredibly exciting. Not every day do you choose to go on an expedition that will alter and improve your life, forever!

It does not matter if you train alone, in a group or if you attend retreats, seminars or practice with resources such as books and videos, or all of these methods. I have found that your first step on the martial arts path is refinement, which is looking at your ability with scrutiny alongside support from leaders and peers in martial arts to continually improve what you practice. In addition, a few simple applications or preventative methods that are adaptable to several circumstances will give you confidence and a degree of control in the cultivation of yourself.

In the next few paragraphs we demonstrate three simple applications that can be studied and practised in any environment. They provide straightforward preventative methods requiring little to none martial art knowledge; although, a deeper capability can alter how you apply them for your benefit. The reason for these beginning steps to martial art proficiency, as far as IG is concerned, is simply to learn a few easy-to-use techniques that feel natural and will give you a good feeling about defending yourself. This will enable you to gain confidence in what you practice.

The primary physical weapon or tool for a martial artist in the case of IG is the punch.

If self-mastery is one of your goals, then knowing the psychology of oneself will be imperative. In addition, refinement is a word that will be forever with the martial artist in their quest for continuous self-improvement. It is ironic that after years of training and personal investigation of your inner world, you may find that refinement and a few choice techniques or principles may be all that is required to become proficient and safe, despite many training methods taking you down a long path of technical development. We shall let time decide this fate as we now focus on the beginning or refocusing of your path.

Time should always be spent refining the tools that are the fundamental principles and building blocks to your skills and martial arts proficiency. My suggestion to you would be refining the IG tools as explained later in this chapter whilst learning other aspects of your particular training. Exposure to many different ways of martial arts may appear disloyal, but we are free to discover what is best for our cultivation – this is the way of self-understanding.

My personal view is that exposure is the key; it was for this reason that I found my own cultivation to be my way. Let me also explain that exposure does not have to mean train in as many different arts as you can. Remember, IG's goal and mission is to view the full spectrum of your capability as a human being. So, expose yourself to what is necessary for you to understand. I personally spent my final eight years of formal training in several methods of traditional Japanese and sport martial arts before I left to venture my own ability. This was due to there being a great exposure of various arts, principles and ideas. I include this fact to emphasise that exposure is not a matter of trying every art you can find, although it may be necessary to do this. The point is to expose yourself to the moment where you find what you need and, more importantly, what you do not need on your own path.

To follow are a couple of examples to get you started or refocused. These will also expose you to the IG principle of a few choice and simple techniques that take a short time to learn.

Please remember that the following examples and photos in this book have been presented in a demonstrative manner to show you as clearly as possible what we are discussing. Also, this book is a primer for individuals either embarking on a new path or refocusing their own, so it is important to realise these are starting points that once grasped can lead to further discovery and martial arts prowess.

Learning to escape some of the more common situations builds great confidence and provides a wonderful starting point for one's journey.

From a single collar grab, strike (push for training purposes) with the heel of your palm under the jaw, knocking back the head of your assailant. Simultaneously, you can hold onto the arm that has grabbed you to gain control and add more leverage to accelerate the force of your strike. Continuing with a knee to the groin and jabbing your fingers into the eyes, you can push and move the head here, which adds more control over your adversary. This allows you time to escape or incapacitate the adversary for a time.

From a single wrist grab, strike the thumb joint, which will cause pain to stun your opponent for a moment, and follow swiftly with a decisive kick to the back of the thigh in the hamstring area. Again, you can use your other hand to manipulate and control your attacker. This will afford you time to escape. Even though it is not likely to incapacitate the adversary, it will possibly shock them long enough for your escape.

From a rear bear hug trapping both arms, raise your heel sharply into the groin. In that moment, lean forwards to one side of your body, bringing the kicking knee forwards to give the space to take out the knee/leg with your heel. Even if a strike is not possible with the foot, you can push away from the attacker.

With these three simple movements, you have already begun taking steps on your path and sharing the view of IG to become an exponent in your chosen field. By practising these simple moves and refining one tool, say the straight blast, it puts you at a great advantage in your martial arts voyage. We will explore this later in the chapter. Or, if you have already begun other paths of training, it helps to refocus your efforts. You can use these simple principles to improve and enhance your prowess and current ability.

Physical Maintenance

There are many different areas of fitness and condition training as we look at one's physical maintenance. By which I simply mean the upkeep and maintenance of your physical being. From simple cardiovascular movement like running or swimming to far more specific training that involves flexibility, strength, resistance, etc. I will provide some examples that you can choose to add to your development if you do not already use them.

Exposure to supplementary training and experimentation with your desired outcome in mind is what will help you remain focused on what is relevant to you at this time in your training. Remember, you are responsible for recognising what fits you best at this point in your journey. This would be training specific to you. Training that befits your own personal way will cover a vast range of methods and will change in a dramatic manner throughout your journey.

As a martial artist, it is critical to maintain a degree of cardiovascular fitness. Therefore, exercises that increase your heart rate for a duration of time, such as aerobics like jogging, running, swimming and circuit training, can all be explored. Hiking and scrambling are also great ways to enjoy the outdoors whilst raising and maintaining your level of fitness. Walking is incredibly healthy and good for stamina, but it cannot raise the heart rate sufficiently without resistance. In fact, there are so many exercises that it really is best to explore what you can because there will be different outcomes depending on how you approach it. Some weight training can be altered to act more like cardiovascular work. Slow motion movement and static exercises can also raise the heart rate and deliver a desired outcome for fitness. In IG we have an exercise called Flowing Sensitivity, which accomplishes a similar goal whilst addressing martial art prowess. This is an important point. I mention in this book how IG acts as a catalyst to your development, and much of this is achieved through synergising exercises. You can be working on an exercise that will look at strategic methods, but a byproduct of the exercise could be fitness, flexibility or mental capability.

Along with fitness levels, strength and flexibility in accordance with your martial art journey are also critical. It is imperative for the martial artist to explore their body and find how to leverage it. Range of motion, achieved through different types of stretching, is important and can assist with strength. Stretching is another subject with many methods of approach but is outside the scope of this book. My advice is to approach it with safety in mind and remind yourself you are training to improve and benefit your body. You can do more harm if you do not stretch correctly.

Good exercises for strength are weight-free training such as push-ups, sit-ups, squats and pull-ups. You then want to add resistance to build your strength further. Plyometric training adds intensity as well as isometric training. Weight training and gym equipment are also great supplementary methods that can be geared towards what you want to achieve. Again, there are many types of training. It is a vast subject that should be explored in your own time and with others. You are likely to become quite social from your own studies, as it is important to engage with specialists of different subjects.

In addition, exercises that target balance, breathing and exploring your senses are important. Reflexes, conditioning, posture, awareness and proprioception can all be explored to cultivate your physical and mental prowess. Now I would like to turn our focus towards encouragement. You are empowered to seek out and fill gaps in your own training; not to be told what is or isn't wholly right or wrong for you. Something for you to bear in mind with IG training to help reinforce this point is that we do not spend any time going through warm-up or cooling down drills in a typical training session because this takes time away from learning true martial art skill. Plus, you never know when you will suffer an attack or be required to act fast. Therefore, each IG exponent is encouraged to take this responsibility alone and make sure they are ready prior to and after training. There is no such difference in the eyes of a true martial artist, but this book is aimed at all levels. This does not mean that warming up and the like are ignored or not talked about. In fact, it is looked at in great depth; but it is important for the budding martial artist to explore, take on and learn.

Because this is a path of self-discovery as well as heightened martial arts prowess, it is important to show due care of the instrument – your body as well as your mind. Balance is key to the discovery of what suits you in your present condition; this is the best way to approach training. Therefore, depending on many factors, it may be suitable to increase your fitness with cardiovascular workouts as mentioned before, or it may be better to improve the health of your internal organs and workings. If you have suffered an injury or disability, then a custom way to train what is most important and possible for you will be more beneficial. It can even be a capability that someone has yet to accept is possible. The list goes on. The critical message is self-awareness and to train in accordance with your personal circumstances. Martial artists are trained to be safe and secure in themselves as the main point amongst others, not to become athletes. Unless you train in a sport, then that may change. However, as a martial artist, your first consideration is you as an individual and to train in accordance with that in mind. This is IG's approach.

The importance of this mindset is crucial for a martial artist because you will need to focus on different areas that you wish to improve at different periods of one's cultivation. There are many circumstances, but what I want to convey is that it is not necessary to be the strongest at something or be put off from training because you know others are quicker or fitter. We all have natural gifts and talents. Through the art of IG, one discovers that being capable is not always about being the fastest, the youngest or best at one or two things. Through the journey of becoming capable, the marvellous transformation from martial arts training is soon discovered.

Train in accordance with your personal circumstances. This is the message from The Way of the Internal Gate. What you discover within you far outweighs and outlasts what you perceive outside of you.

Master of One

Becoming skilful with a few simple movements at a time as previously discussed is the crucial point. At the beginning or refocusing of one's training, you will gain confidence through seeing genuine progress in your ability. Rather than trying to learn or do too much too soon, you can be surprised just how much you can learn from a handful of simple movements. This model of training will uncover your temperament towards life as the mental mist begins to settle.

The punch is the primary physical weapon or tool for a martial artist in the case of IG. Perhaps some may argue, martial arts are defensive, why is it not a block or a defensive movement? But before defending it, it's important to understand how one can be attacked first. This is more about the psychology of the attack; we are more than likely not going to be struck in the same way that we cultivate our own attacks. Until this is absorbed, the punch should be practised as often as possible. I am still practising the punch, along with other simple tools like hook and side kick. Manipulating different body types, whilst refining and learning from these simple movements are important to keep razor sharp. With one or two potent moves and tools at your disposal, it is underestimated how prepared you now are for self-preservation. Even by yourself, you may not judge depending on only a handful of moves effective enough to defend your life. However, let IG assure you that you will already be in a strong position of defence and self-preservation.

Once the decision of a tool has been made for cultivation, you should begin with how you move and articulate your body to get the best results from your striking or impact ability. I believe it is important to choose a realistic tool that can adapt to many fighting consequences by applying conflict scenarios in the preservation of your life.

Let us look at the tools of IG for your own journey.

The IG Tools

I feel that striking is essential to grasp. The idea is not to be confined to a few simple methods but allow yourself to breathe into your ability and movement as a whole, physiologically speaking. As mentioned previously, body awareness is essential to understand our ability in issuing ourselves. This is our inherent talent.

The punch and kick are essential tools for the martial artist regardless of your type of training, which may be grappling, studying locks, using redirection of force, and so forth. Even defensive arts need to understand the nature of what kind of attacks to expect. In fact, this knowledge alone gives insight into the grand experience of martial arts education and its diversity. Even if your training emphasises throwing or grappling, this can greatly complement and enhance your skills as much as throwing and grappling can for predominant striking arts. However, striking has the advantage of keeping your adversary at bay, whereas the other two require infighting. Depending on the circumstance of attack such as with weapons or when there are multiple adversaries, this may not be wise in a real situation. To illustrate, try the following:

From a ready position of your choice, have three training partners come at you one by one and perform any technique(s) you prefer to each one. They can be armed or unarmed, and you are to use close-quarter grappling and fighting as mentioned above. Now, let your adversaries come at you all at once and try the same close-quarter grappling techniques. You will find that you are more likely to be crowded in this real-life scenario, so your chosen or preferred technique, instead of keeping some distance to ward off or escape, will possibly tie you up and help your adversaries.

It is important to become aware and mindful of the obvious in your self-discovery and voyage in martial arts. Everything, depending on its circumstance and intent, will show advantages and disadvantages. Rather than persuading ourselves why we do this or that training, it is best to be impartial and look for what benefits and downfalls could improve all training in any situation.

The IG tools and indeed the movement of the martial artist are used in every inch of one's being, but we start with the extremities and learn its intricacies to refine and cultivate. Diligent training in the punch and kick are core to a martial artist using IG's approach. You learn one movement well with a solid understanding, and then it is time to expand your repertoire once the principles are part of you. As a practitioner of IG, you always keep in mind the cultivation of your core IG tools. The principles of these will carry into every other part of your development for the future, along with harvesting new ideas and tools for the budding martial artist.

IG's philosophy is to be limitless with the entirety of oneself and use the whole being to preserve one's life. This may appear like a vague expression, but it is only meant to aid you in maintaining a flexible and unperturbed mind. In the heat of the moment, you will be issuing your movement in any way to preserve your life. Due to your genetic make-up and physical constitution, it is also recognised that using reference points, such as the way your body needs to move and the ability to identify this and return to it through self-enquiry as a reference, are required to aid cultivation. For this reason, IG has four main tools that help the individual to grow and develop the principles of striking. Only these four tools are necessary. After some time, the individual is then encouraged to develop their own tools with guidance as appropriate. Remember, this is your own voyage of martial arts using IG as the vehicle to attain your ability. In IG, the primary focus is always the person. It respects the cultivation and uniqueness of each human being and their growth.

Let us now look at the primary IG tools in more detail.

The superior weapon of IG is the straight blast darting out like a viper with a refined power that can become equal to a full swing. Again, it is not just arm power but also the body due to the legs and body playing an intricate part. Without this, the straight blast has less advantage. In saying that, it is potent in close quarters once a level of refinement is accomplished. It is all about circumstance and addressing the immediate situation. In fact, this sums up IG in simple terms. Refinement is the important word here for the martial artist.

To execute the straight blast, begin in a ready posture comfortable for you. The straight blast favours the lead hand in any posture you begin with. Whichever is in front, that is the hand you will execute in preference. Although, it is possible to do this with the hand closest to you. It is determined by the circumstance – such as knowing there is not enough leverage for the lead hand to have effect, so you use the hand nearest to you because it has more room to deliver. Exerting pressure into the floor and using the joints of your body, harmonise and coordinate the power so the force becomes a synergy and is directed to focus on shooting out of the structured arm. The intricacies of this movement lie in the rotation and snap of the body moving similar to a whip, thus allowing the force to build momentum through your body to exert at the moment of impact. The lead hand of this strike always returns and hovers once again at the ready.

Below is an application of the straight blast.

In a standoff situation, the aggressor lunges with a lead hand attack that the IG exponent avoids whilst remaining covered and poised for a counter-attack. As the aggressor continues the assault, the IG exponent meets them head-on with the power of the straight blast coupled with the momentum of the aggressor's attack.

The Blast

The blast is a continuation from the straight blast, but it is not merely a case of strike, strike and strike in an aimless manner. The cultivation of one's physical being is unique in this application because the dedicated focus of the straight blast is further intensified with one's mental ability. The blast is applied with continuous effort and stamina requiring mental and physical unity that must be achieved and sustained for it to have any true effect, along with a good knowledge of your adversary in that moment. Not that you know your adversary on a personal level, but it means you are acutely observing their every move physically and intentions through psychology or strategy of attack. As you're launching your strikes, your instinct is feeling out what is left open by your adversary and where you can take advantage or potentially create one. Knowledge of your adversary here means keen reading of them, the circumstance and your environment. Focus is key to the blast.

In executing the blast, take up your ready position again and make a straight blast with your lead hand. Immediately follow up with the same from your rear hand, and so on for between six to ten strikes. At first, do not put too much power into this because you can strain your arms. This awareness of injuring yourself is important to your development in martial arts as it raises the intensity on a gradual basis and lets your body tell you when it is time to move again.

Remaining poised and balanced throughout, the blast is exploded out in front of you.

Although the picture demonstrates the blast in an upright posture, it can and will begin to form more peculiar angles of entry on your opponent.

The Hook Kick

The hook kick uses a variety of angles of attack relating to the choice of target in the moment. These can range from areas of the legs, the ribs or the head. Hooking the kick uses the rotation of the leg at the hip joint. In IG, this kick has a quick and alarming presence like the straight blast. With refinement, it can dart out at the opponent with little warning. Depending upon your attacker, this can widen the gap and create uncertainty and hesitation in their movements. Although the hook kick is fast and depends on its speed and surprise, it can still have a strong impact. This is a great asset to the IG exponent and martial artist who choose to refine and cultivate this formidable kick in their arsenal. Using accuracy and timing are imperative to its function and effect.

To execute the hook kick starting from your ready position, shuffle your back foot close to your front foot. Using that momentum, bring the knee of your front leg into a chambered position. Then rotate the knee from the hip joint and strike using the shin.

The rotation is the focal point in the beginning phases. Once this principle is absorbed, the kick is practised with all the various angles possible.

The Side Kick

The side kick is a strong and powerful tool that serves as a deadly attack. It also keeps your opponent off-balance when they try to invade your personal space, so it becomes a guard in your defence. This kick bursts out at your adversaries on either their attack or as one of your own. The potency of this movement is in your own control. The more you refine it to a higher level, the greater the impact this vicious weapon will carry. The side kick is a menacing tool, and one in particular that I and other IG exponents have found to disrupt and worry an adversary's attack.

Sideways kicking uses the momentum created from clever footwork, like the hook kick, by putting you in a side-on position that travels into the target.

In executing the side kick, bring your weight on to the front leg and turn your front hip towards your target. Next, exert pressure into the floor and bring your rear foot close to your front leg. Then the knee of your front leg comes up so you are now balancing on your rear foot. As you chamber your front leg and bring up your knee, you turn your hip slightly and kick out with your heel as the weapon towards its target.

It is important to mention that to get the most out of these strikes, although they are effective in their own way, footwork will enhance and further cultivate their application.

In the following example, you will see how the IG tools form a natural flow from one to the other. The sequence below was unplanned and occurred in a spontaneous moment, except the initial side kick movement, which again demonstrates the effectiveness and flow of these IG tools.

These are the four primary IG tools that I personally train in and consider beneficial to any martial artist regardless of their chosen study. I also believe that these are the only requirements to infuse the principles before developing your own tools for your future martial arts voyage. After such time and cultivation, you can expand and learn to use your unique ability, diversely. How to use the totality of oneself to then implement and issue your power is of greatest importance over knowing more and more moves in IG's view.

In all the tools you will notice the attention to stay alert, ready for your continuation if it is needed. The blast truly emphasises this at high intensity.

The IG tools are a foundation to your commencement of martial arts training in IG. They are used to preserve your life in the variety of situations that Mother Nature and humanity offers to us. As previously mentioned, awareness is the key to recognition and cultivation; therefore, maintain awareness of your environment in which your training occurs. In other words, in IG we want you to become aware of the different psychological impacts of what occurs around us as well as within us.

If grappling, throwing, locks or direction of the force is your chosen study, and you have not yet considered the basic principles of striking, then I suggest looking at the IG tools and experimenting with them. Depending on one's way or characteristics, a particular method of fighting will always suit that individual at the outset of one's martial arts voyage. However, if you are a seasoned martial artist, you will be able to pick something out of great use with the knowledge of your current training.

Challenging ourselves is how we can grow. IG believes in exposure, which is why the philosophy is to encompass the full spectrum of the human being. This is a gigantic task, but self-discovery becomes the focal point with this approach. You can use this principle to upgrade your whole being and become a better individual too.

As will be discussed later in this volume, it is not what you do but how you do it that is of greatest importance.

IG Tools

IG Tools are the building blocks in the application of IG. They are taught as a transferable skill because once learnt they can be applied in any situation, be it a punch, kick, grab, throw or whatever the circumstance is. In learning the basic tools, the focus is placed on the smaller motions just as much as the larger ones. For example, with the punch you learn to use your legs, feet, hips, knees, back, spine, even your neck to a certain extent, and then your arms, not just your upper body.

4th Gate IG Exponent

On Your Guard

The approach IG takes with the guard is to have constant awareness and mental strength as your state of mind, rather than thinking of or adopting certain positions or postures. I will expand briefly on the mental aspect here before we continue with the physical. There are some situations when you will be distracted or not aware, so your awareness may not always pick up on a potential incident. However, your mental strength is developed to compose yourself as quickly as possible. In the majority of circumstances, your training in IG will develop a way to sense and become aware of something. This then becomes your true guard as you continue to hone this skill.

Physically, as a martial artist, you will want to refine yourself. Therefore, you may want to begin from a certain position and then experiment with others. However, whichever way you start in IG, you emphasise the ability to move in whatever circumstance you find yourself in. This is where your footwork can make your tools work for you too. The core to having a strong guard is looking at the natural mechanics of the human being and the individual's unique ability. Some of the IG exercises help you to detect with speed and then cultivate further this inherent ability we all possess. Sometimes we are psychologically hindered due to what appears to be a lack of structure, believing we need to be in a ready stance or super alert to our surroundings for our guard to be effective. IG is aware of this and any other preconceived ideas that could potentially obstruct your flow. It trains to meet this head-on so the individual becomes more capable in the heat of the moment.

From the perspective of IG, being on your guard is to use the mind and instinct to facilitate and then act in accordance with the situation at hand. Rather than reacting to the situation, it is a response to one. Depending on the situation you find yourself in, the type of attacker you are up against, the environment and also your own willpower at that time, you may find that taking up a guard is appropriate for protection. Or you may wish to lure them into a thought you have, such as feigning being drunk or a severe illness, then protecting yourself with aggressive precision and surprise. Or, if you know you have been 'picked' for an attack, lead your adversary (or adversaries) to an area you know better if the situation is there to take advantage. There are many occasions where verbal interactions can change and control the dynamic of a situation and defuse the intent.

Likewise, there are also social tactics that can alter the original intended outcome. An example is becoming aware of being targeted. In the best circumstances, move out into a crowded area where socially you are less inclined to be attacked or you can hide in the crowd. This is not a guaranteed strategy as it depends on the nature of attack and the intention. If your attacker or attackers are determined, a crowd will be a delaying tactic but not necessarily a social deterrent. In addition, you may find it inappropriate to assume any kind of posture if there is no time to take one up, but being alert and instinctive will keep you in the best frame of mind to preserve your life and assess the situation.

Having the ability to monitor levels of stress adhering to the situation and internal factors like your own emotional escalation, mental stress or external factors are also an important part of the guard. This includes observing your adversaries breathing and posturing as well as recognising social tendencies within your environment, such as someone attacking and showing off in front of their partners or friends and how this may be escalating.

A good example of stress levels is to think of a time when someone has acted negatively towards you when driving or you have witnessed 'road rage' (a term only recently coined). It is very interesting to note that many peoples' stress levels are heightened when on the road. There are some alarming statistics about this that are worth looking up. Essentially, focus, awareness and full concentration are key to driving safely; but these factors alter when there is a dip in concentration or a distraction. There are several emotions that come under scrutiny and many people 'lose their cool' due to external factors.

Below are four examples to highlight some of these points where different circumstances will require their own response dependant on several factors. Each photo is a snapshot of these different situations that could lead to varying states of mind and awareness.

Your consciousness can also alter depending on factors such as the time of day, what you were doing prior to the moment of potential conflict, your level of energy and many more possible reasons.

How do you intend to move and respond in everyday circumstances? How do you reduce your chances of being caught off guard? When learning to move in IG, you will discover how best to increase your power and output by adopting the living principles herein to upgrade your skills and prowess. This philosophy provides one with a choice of cultivation along with freedom. These are two essential elements of the martial artist. In other words, it is not necessary to adopt the exact pictures you see, but to apply some of the fundamental ideas and principles and relate to the situation at hand. Thus, you become alive in the moment.

To be on your guard is to adhere to the concepts behind your actions and to be creative in using your wit and instincts. There is no rigidity as you become natural and in constant motion, meaning your awareness to your instincts always flows as you begin to tap into this vast human resource.

Footwork

The essence of footwork is to be capable of moving in any direction at any time to your advantage or protection. There is a lot that comes down to controlling the space in a face-to-face encounter, and your footwork can help to dictate this. Rather than thinking of a set of steps or a specific way of moving or placing your feet, IG sets out to encourage the individual to become free of movement, so to speak, and to understand his or her own origin of power. This then becomes absorbed by that person and the body becomes knowledgeable in how to instinctively move to issue the most power in any given situation. Although there are many set ways to increase one's output of power, it surprises most how unique the individual can move to issue their own from a variety of angles.

The principles behind footwork and guarding are interrelated in the philosophy of IG. The ability of free movement and thought is important as we can never be certain of the circumstance we will find ourselves in. Therefore, it becomes a principle of survival to attune ourselves accordingly and make the best of where we find ourselves, much as we do in everyday life. Thus, footwork in IG is not dictated by a set of patterns for foot movement. Instead, with deliberate means, we put ourselves under duress through exposure to find how best to articulate our bodies to produce the most effect at that moment. It all comes back to understanding yourself and where the origin of your power is at that critical point. Body awareness and the skill to issue your ability in that moment is the crucial aspect.

I hope it has now become clear that IG sets out to explore your entire being whilst leaving nothing unturned. It is always asking, always searching and, therefore, always discovering. Questioning oneself and one's ability becomes far more important than asking another how they think you are doing. But this does not disparage the importance of guidance, such as these books or a guide in martial arts, because self-knowledge is the solution to your cultivation in the end. I believe that ultimately, you are responsible for your growth and you need to be the single ingredient to push for it.

Paying attention to our natural physical heritage and keeping an open, flexible mind with the spirit of learning is fundamental to expanding our insight and advancing our ability.

The Way It Is Done: Cultivation

As the old adage goes, 'it's not what you do, but how you do it'. This could not be truer in the application of IG and its approach to martial arts training and, in turn, the cultivation of the individual. There is no limit to your creativity in your ascension to martial arts prowess. Remember, there is no right or wrong here, but there is always a way to improve and better yourself. IG has no hard or fast rules for what it uses to cultivate the individual, and it will try to make use of anything to hand.

The accompaniment of equipment is vital to IG practitioners because they are used as a barometer to measure the tools for one's own improvement and ability. They help with the direction of that individual and their growth.

Following are some examples of how pad work is used to improve and enhance IG's straight blast. The exercise is not limited in any way, and you can use any and all tools for this training.

Be patient and the results will come. Use your awareness to gain knowledge and trust your instincts. Our thoughts often become a hindrance as we intellectualise what we are doing and think too much instead of allowing instinct to flow. Complex training can often be the result of overthinking, so awareness of this is key in your training.

I always say, 'Let your body do some of the thinking for you.' This expression is to encourage and build the trust in oneself. This is IG.

Focus mitts are used in IG to cultivate accuracy, speed, resistance, reaction, distance, response and body feel. The example opposite demonstrates the cultivation of the straight blast's speed and accuracy.

A kick shield can not only be used to cultivate kicks. In this example, the focus of the straight blast is on the development of depth, impact, power and proper body structure. By driving into the shield with vigour, you become aware of how to position your body for a structured strike. You can see in this photo that the whole force of the body is invoked to issue power.

In the example above, a game is played where each exponent tries to strike the other's pad whilst adjusting the body at the same time to avoid their pad getting struck. This training helps to cultivate speed, timing, accuracy, distance and judgement. Footwork and body movement are emphasised to accomplish this goal. At first, the pads are held as illustrated above. However, you and your partner can move the pad around at any time as you advance, which makes an interesting way to grow with the attributes mentioned here.

Focus Mitts Reaction Exercise

This exercise cultivates timing and reaction as your training partner presses the focus mitt to their body and you stand ready to punch the pad. Without warning, they open out their arm to expose the mitt for you to strike. Begin with simple placement of the pad, and then vary the angles and distance of the target to improve.

After a time when your proficiency is developed, you can vary your strikes and find out how capable you are with strikes from different angles that have the same level of consistency. It is essential not to limit creativity or hinder progress, so looking for ways to evolve is the natural method to train.

Equipment, as shown here, is vital to your practice as it will encourage cultivation and also measure and improve whether alone or with a partner. You are only limited by your imagination, so concentrate and focus on how you can cultivate yourself with the training so as not to become stagnant.

Every training aid has a unique purpose, in the same way that every weapon has a unique characteristic. Armed with the living principles, go out and discover how to develop and learn about yourself.

Question for Cultivation

What angle of punching feels most natural to you? Straight, hooking arm or rotating arm motion? Front arm, rear, from above, below or sideways?

Refining Your Skills

Cultivation implies natural growth, whereas refinement is what balances it with control and precision leading you to martial art prowess. The same as we have natural instincts, which at times would be antisocial to act out, they are balanced by appropriate learnt behaviour to act more social in society, like patience, manners or being civil. We are not born saying please, waiting and then saying thank you afterwards. As toddlers you see something you want and just grab it from someone or somewhere with not a care of the consequence, and then you complain if you cannot have it.

You now begin to ask yourself questions: How can I improve my tools? How can I develop speed, timing, power, accuracy, etc.? We then take an objective view of ourselves using awareness to see how we are now in the present and making mental notes of this. Being honest, we ask ourselves individual questions and focus on each one separately. Always keep in mind the purpose, which is to improve the totality of our bodies and self.

For example, we first want our tools to be effective. So how can we put more power into this tool? Let's use the punch to start. We begin to move our bodies and ask if there is anything obstructive or uncomfortable in our body movement. If we punch with sheer muscle power that comes from the arm alone, we can use the rest of our body weight to add more to the tool by coordinating our movement. Using kinaesthesia, which is to feel and 'see' in your mind the direction your body moves, your structure and internal awareness or focus of delivery, we increase the ability to generate more power and can harness its force more efficiently. This is how we will develop and grow.

Let us look at the straight blast and ways to improve how we use it for self-preservation. Remember, you apply this approach to any weapon or movement of your choice as you feel the living principles being absorbed into your individual approach.

In this example, we shall begin from a guarded position and look at our hand movements, breaking down the movement and where we are at present.

The lead hand hovers in front of the body like the first line in battle or even as a scout observing its enemies' movements.

Shooting out to its chosen target, the power is directed through the arm.

By analysing the technical aspects of the movement above and focusing on this tool (not considering the situational or environmental impact, but to explore your movement alone for now), the elbow points down to provide an extra surge of power using structure. This is another principle in IG where the structure takes precedence over power at this stage of cultivation. This alignment strengthens the tool as the forearm to the knuckles carries your force with the shoulder behind it, and then you want to gain a full alignment of the body to issue power.

In reality, when faced with the pressure of genuine violent attacks, we are not fortunate enough to be in place and ready for it. This is why IG looks at this training as what it is: refinement, not reality. Punching with arm strength alone can be powerful, and it is more than possible to increase, but what about increasing this power by including the whole of your body? How can you coordinate and increase body power, not just arm power? With this kind of honest self-questioning and examination, you investigate using proprioception, kinaesthesia and your own awareness, which is built through your training.

The balls of the feet are pressed into the floor, starting a chain reaction of upward force and creating a spring to exert power. This is then directed through the joints of your body and channelled out of your arm.

The refinements above are for one weapon in your arsenal and can be transferable. They will only be limited by yourself. These questions and principles are applied to every other aspect of your training. Once you have begun to cultivate and refine your ideas and weapons, you will want to further this training by focusing on another development, such as speed, the economy of motion or accuracy, etc. Most training crosses a few areas of development, but you need to give the time and quality to each element of your ever-growing martial arts prowess to cultivate with genuine results.

Harmonising with the Opponent(s)

You will want to test your skills as they come to the surface. This leads into the application through training with others. You will discover throughout each subject touched upon in this volume that there is time cultivated in each period of the living principles. This book sets out to provide a clear progression, but it is your choice and free will to decide where and what you begin with, continue to refine, understand or wish to adopt from these pages. This is to go into your own self-cultivation and training. In your experience, refining your tool/weapon and harmonising with your opponents are two important principles to achieve genuine skill and understanding.

To harmonise with the opponent does not necessarily mean allowing their movement to dictate or that you have to fit in with something they do. With this principle, it serves as a much grander meaning in that you are studying and, sometimes due to the urgency of the attack, instinctively finding out about your adversary. Looking at the words and phrase 'to harmonise with the opponent', we may begin to think about blending or moving in a smooth or gentle way within their actions. Listening to one's instinct, it can also suggest understanding both physically and mentally your attacker/s and the environment you are in at that moment. To cultivate this training, the initial emphasis is on a total physical level using footwork that, once proficient, leads instinctively on to total bodywork.

Let us say that we want to refine the punch again and learn how to harmonise this tool. How can we use this strike to great effect against our adversary's attack as a means of self-preservation? Remember, we train against any way the human can and will assault another human. This is a fundamental basis of how your technique can improve by continuing to ask questions that expose yourself to further insight. Everything begins in the mind, so it is up to us to cultivate it from there.

The following two examples are taken from the guard examples we discussed earlier to illustrate the principle of harmonising with the opponent.

36

An exponent leans against a wall as an assailant creeps up from behind to attack them. They grab the exponent to pull, gain leverage and then off-balance them as they expose a baton. Responding with instinct, the exponent kicks back instinctively using the wall as a balancing aid and increasing force. They lean forwards slightly to create distance whilst causing pain to reduce and hopefully avoid the intended strike. The exponent continues the advantage which off-balances and opens an opportunity for another strike against the assailant and gives more time to escape.

The exponent remains in a seated position as an assailant kicks to their head. The exponent drops instinctively, raising their arm to protect against the strike and hold up the leg of the assailant as the exponent sees an opening for an attack to the assailant's supporting leg. Not wanting to remain on the floor, the exponent continues the momentum of attack with another kick whilst keeping the assailant off-balance and controlling them to end their ability and want to fight further.

Again, these are principles and as such can be adapted to many areas of your training. So, movement is the key to the principle, whilst your awareness and self-discovery are the essence to understand it. Bear these words in mind as you further explore and practice harmonising with your opponents.

Reality of Fighting – Conflict

One aspect of training that can be overlooked and difficult to gauge is to know what is possible realistically, even when carrying out a slow movement or performing an action step by step. Without the ability to foresee the possible realities of a situation, your movement and ideas will be ineffective when applying it to actual conflict. For example, when approaching the pad work we started with, you cultivate your ability by thinking about where the opponent would be as you go to strike. Like a strong brew of tea, you want to infuse this into your training. Rather than seeing it as a part of training, it must become your training to further your abilities.

Remember, how you move reflects how you think, and how you think reflects how you move. For a martial artist, it is important to work at a deep physical level here. You train mind as well, but for now what counts is physical expression. Learning to inject this principle and feeling into your own training will give a sense of truthfulness in what you do.

The principle, 'reality of fighting' is what keeps your art alive, along with expressing sincerely.

Simple and Effective

Some people believe simplicity to be the highest level in art, and I truly understand this. In regards to the physical application of martial arts, for the exponent of IG when under attack, the quickest and simplest option makes the most sense. What defines this is the weakest area closest to you. For example, the eyes are primary targets because this area will be sensitive and a weak part of your opponent no matter who they are. Although, it will always be vital to observe if this is most appropriate as you evaluate the circumstance. However, every movement you make is a strategy all of its own. All things depend on this circumstance, and there is no way of formulating or creating a template for it. As far as self-expression is concerned, you cannot copyright a movement. Martial arts are a realistic and living art, so if you are near the eyes it will be a prime target for you to attack. However, another target would need to be assessed in less than a second should you not be near the eyes in the heat of the moment. This is how to cultivate 'simple and effective' in martial arts. It requires great skill to truly apply this principle, which means time in training and study.

The Subject of Anatomy

In Chapter 1 section titled 'Through Self-Defence to Self-Discovery', the self-defence element is used as a way/medium to expose or access your self-discovery. We apply this same principle of thought for 'The Subject of Anatomy' by using body weaknesses as a way/medium to subdue opponents. We use this method to guide us where we want to go. In this case, to understand the human anatomy will better enhance our chances of preserving our lives. The better this is understood, the greater the chance of everyone being saved in a situation, even though your life must be your priority. With a myriad of situations, this knowledge will help tantamount in the direction you will want to take.

There is a lot of content on nerve strikes, pressure points, meridian striking, dim mak and so on, which can be a complicated subject as well as time consuming. However, you can immediately realise the benefit, both martial and health wise, in these kinds of subjects. Conversely, it is important to know that certain body parts cannot be protected without great ingenuity, and certainly not all the time. IG's outlook is built on urgency and understanding in response to the genuine threat we face in the world today and our future.

As for the study of these arts, firstly it is important to realise that this type of knowledge is not necessary to disarm an assailant. This is not to disparage you as there are benefits to its training, but it is to inform you of IG's outlook on martial arts application and training. Secondly, it can put you in even more danger, much like any martial arts knowledge without genuine guidance, because you can think that striking certain areas may make them fall over. What I want to convey in this book is that we are all individual and some points work on some and not on others. Thirdly, this type of technical striking requires extreme pinpoint accuracy in extremely intense circumstances. Finally, knowing about the points and reaching them or applying your knowledge of them in conflict is different. Great care and caution are required with these vast subjects. Now, I'm not denying or discouraging that there is a place for this training in martial arts, but balance is the key. Anatomy is vital. The more you understand and can apply this knowledge, the better.

However, a simple fact I would like to mention is that weak points are exactly that: areas or points of the body that are weak or cause damage to the human body. We have obvious weak points, such as eyes and groin, because these areas cannot build muscle or protection from damage when struck. Interestingly, this study can lead to a comprehensive, detailed understanding of yourself and others. For the IG exponent, such as myself, it is critical to know certain facts on the subject of anatomy and to make sure they are second nature before any further knowledge is researched.

IG's concerns are self-preservation and self-realisation, so there will be priorities that you value important during the time you train as you move along your path. A lot of mine is spent in self-discovery. As for the subject of anatomy, this is a great study of weaknesses and strengths. I would like to share another thought with you on this: broadly speaking, a weakness is anything that puts your opponent at a disadvantage. Consider anatomy and its place in your training like your study of energy and martial arts prowess. Please study this deeply and remember this as you are cultivating, as I have mentioned in the 'Physical Maintenance' section at the start of this chapter.

The Game of Distance

Your interpretation to what distance means is a great catalyst to your martial arts prowess. Knowing what distance is in measurement alone is only the tip of the iceberg in IG. In other words, your instinctive awareness of 'ability in the moment' needs to be cultivated. Distance can now infer insight, which can only be acquired with a calm and focused mind as you put faith into your own imagination.

Here is an example of using a simple attack to improve your knowledge and instinctive awareness of distance:

40

There are two sides of learning to this exercise: the one attacking and the other receiving. Looking at the receiver's role, the attacker starts with a distant punch such as a swing from the rear hand (as above). Then, the distance of attack is shortened to increase the difficulty of the receiver's ability to time their movement. After this is explored, the exponent needs to make space or distance to create opportunity. Speed is then added at each stage before cultivating further. In the following stages, the attacker reduces their distance until striking from a short distance.

The exercise demonstrated above can be carried out with an infinite variety of attacks to upgrade your knowledge. Take this idea and grow it with your own thoughts. Try this with multiple types of attacks and discover for yourself what angles create the most pressure on you. This will enable you to uncover and gauge what comes natural and what does not.

This is your path to self-discovery, through the expedition of martial art prowess.

Explore these exercises with the spirit of learning and endurance as you expose yourself to further cultivation. This will lead to greater insight into your own being. Here's a question for you to ponder: how would we use the attacking role in the above exercise to learn and cultivate?

Below is another exercise to help judging distance with your instincts and spatial awareness. In IG we call this practice 'perception'. This demonstrates the beginning aspects of it.

Please note the practice of training in various environments. This is part of the wonderful heritage of martial arts training. Everything can have a different feel and, indeed, experience when carried out under different conditions. As a martial artist studying self-preservation, it is your responsibility to expose yourself to any and all circumstances in your training. Don't confine yourself and your training skills to a room that remains ideal for a comfortable fall or take down. If there are no weather conditions, such as being on slippery ground, it could hinder a favourite technique. By practising on uneven grounds, in different conditions, you breathe life into your true skill and your ability grows. In IG it is imperative to train in nature and take advantage of what I have personally heard from people as reasons not to train. Your mental growth will develop an altered perspective with these experiences. This enhances both physical and mental skills as you learn to respond to strange instances, thus becoming less perturbed under stressful situations.

The following and final exercises on distance in this volume are used in IG to increase distance, strategy, timing, response and many further skills. This exercise can be performed in any environment to enhance your senses and human capacity to discover what different world conditions can offer to gain further understanding. All of this is directly connected to the fundamentals of martial arts.

The following is a demonstration of the same exercise performed indoors using a different tool to develop keen distance and insight.

Please try these exercises to see what you discover for yourself. The secret to gaining true insight from them is not to look at the exercises themselves for guidance, but to venture in your own ability and cultivation. This is the root premise of IG.

Accuracy Implies Intention

Although this is straightforward, it can take time to cultivate a natural instinctive level. Basically, referring to our application of martial art prowess, we train to become accurate. As previously mentioned, being accurate under intense pressure is not enough because accuracy requires deep focus whilst many factors occur. To become accurate when dealing with the infusion of your other training requires your intention to be cultivated. Applying this in real world circumstances is difficult unless you train to become accustomed to it.

For example, how do you remain accurate at blinding speed at the onset of being attacked? The intention, which is fuelled by the human will, is to be cultivated. This develops human character and a strong will.

Accuracy Exercise

Create a movement requiring one or two targets on your opponent. Starting with a specific attack and eventually becoming a random attack on you. Whatever it is, let your opponent build up their attacking speed and intensity. Use your awareness to discover how you apply yourself, what obstructs you from meeting your targets and how you handle it as it builds.

Become the Weapon, Become Alive

With your intentions beginning to flow through in your endeavours, allow this to infuse your totality and expression of your aims. Once this is possible, you can also learn the skill of masking this intent. But, for now, we deal with our clear intentions. Plainly speaking, this is a refinement of yourself in your movement, whatever form it takes. When you strike, you must become that strike and let it thunder from your core. Become the instrument with the clarity of thought in that moment.

This philosophy can also be adapted to how you conduct yourself through life and help to maintain an inner understanding, which will lead to emotional well-being through the expression of oneself.

Let this feeling flow into all your other endeavours and become alive.

There Is No Limit

It would be ideal for all who train in any subject to embrace the idea of no limit, not only in martial arts. Briefly, I would like to say that you will discover any gaps in restriction when finding what truly is or is not possible. It is also important to remember the journey is individual. With no restrictive thoughts and a focus on you as a single being, you can clearly find answers to yourself and absorb what is truly necessary for you. Creativity is inherent to all humans. We are born with this creativity and although we all express it differently, some more than others, the dynamism of this instinct exists in us all and is the source of no limitation.

Start with these questions: How can I have no restrictive thoughts? In what way can I improve this? Could this work? Your journey has now begun in this principle. Just remember that creativity and reducing your boundaries does not always mean a radical way of thinking. The flexible mind of the martial artist is key to understanding this particular topic.

What About Qi, Energy?

This part is a suggestion and something for you to ponder during times of uncertainty on this esoteric subject in martial arts called energy. IG concentrates on force first of all. It is tangible, effective and able to be used immediately. I have seen many good martial artists become consumed with the subject of Qi, including myself when I was younger. Focusing on it, you can lose time on other important growth aspects of your being and waste valuable time in training.

I am friends with many Tai Qi Quan and Qigong practitioners, including other specific energy-related methods, as well as other artists who study this area of martial arts and health training, all of whom have a different take on energy. This in itself adds a degree of confusion to an already complex subject. I have looked into and explored this kind of training for some time, so I speak with experience. I was attracted to the esoteric side of martial arts in my late teens, believing in magical feats and trying to learn them. I found out the hard way because if there were secrets, I needed help discovering them. There were none that I found. I believe that if something natural exists and you train towards it, then there shall be an awakening. However, what I found was that the real mysteries or secrets were not channelling this mysterious power known as energy. You need to look inward, into your own mind, and discover the ingredients that make up you. Like a secret family recipe handed down over the years and protected by the business, some ingredients are obvious but others aren't quite identifiable.

You are the magnificence in this world; there's nothing more believable or tangible. Learning your unique nature is ultimate, compared to pushing someone twenty yards or leaping ten feet in the air with mysterious energy. In any case, the right circumstances would be needed for their true effects. A lot of demonstrations used to showcase someone's ability with energy have now been shown to work with little to no knowledge of these arts. It is the use of scientific explanations. It is important to be aware of this and compare both viewpoints.

Overall, energy is our natural capacity and capability. We use it every second of every day. It is around you from external factors and powers you within, even beyond trials where you are exhausted in extreme circumstances. The word energy is ambiguous and covers many angles, so training in it requires a degree of faith and specific direction. If this is a subject you aim to invest a great deal of time in, then I would only say be as sure as possible about what you hope to achieve with it. Or at least have an idea of the real value that not only provides great impetus in your studies but also defines the reason. This suggestion comes from my own experience and time put into such things, as now I realise there was time wasted that could have been better utilised.

I value personal time and learning how best to use it with great importance. As your time in training cultivates, your vision and perception shifts – or I could say expands. Due to our distracted mind, we are not commonly aware of our physical nature until called for, such as injury or a need to focus. All people need to do is increase mind awareness of one's physicality with the goal of making one's body alive.

As conditionings and distractions impinge and block our true nature from the expression, we simply need to reverse this by releasing and infusing our nature. Thus, we become our own antithesis; we can only cure ourselves. This is the core of martial arts. We continuously look outside of our beings to help fix problems. This is understandable, as we all need to find a route or a way that is suitable and applicable to us. But the true root of all things exists within us. I eventually came to this realisation and perception physically whilst training. I used to be concerned with external attacks from my opponents. Then I stumbled upon my weakness; my martial arts path led me to my inner opponent. If you want to achieve self-mastery, you will need to come face-to-face with the cold truth that hides deep within your soul. Physical ability will stand you in good stead when attacked by someone else. However, when facing that which cannot be seen and ultimately has a grip on your core existence, physical ability will be limited through psychology.

The subject of one's energy is important and must be studied, but do not become consumed by it. As a caution, only train in what you have faith in; doing something blindly can be costly when we broach the subject of our time. Remember to balance out your training and learn about your physicality to realise your energy. This gives the subject something tangible and real to work with when carried out this way. As your mind is, your body expresses and your energy is the medium.

In my view, the real life force exists as a driving component in our biology using fluids as its carrier. It is responsible for the core of our state of existence, taking on a larger scale than just single beings. It is beyond the scope of this book to discuss in great detail, and it does not rest solely in the realm of martial arts, but I will say that there is a life force within us that can be altered over time through our biological state.

My personal and honest hope is that one day a clear path to this becomes evident, as I believe it will change the course of humanity. This life force is the conduit for heightening and upgrading our consciousness; it is not a purpose for demonstrations from specific individuals who have trained in energy types of arts. This energy's goal is not for martial arts performance but for a greater good in humanity.

Here are some observations to consider: The increased tingling sensation or heat that often comes from exercises where you concentrate energy in the hands or other body parts is due to an increase of fluids to that area. When you sleep on your arm and wake up with what's commonly known as a 'dead arm', the reverse occurs and slows or halts fluid circulation. Some of the famous death strikes known in martial art circles are areas of the body that trigger a mechanism to halt fluids such as blood circulation when struck. The reverse to all the above is made when the intention is to heal. In regards to healing, all bodily fluids and systems, including the health of the mind, are involved to strengthen the make-up of our immune system.

The greater awareness and sensitivity to your life force and entire being that you have, the more you will be able to apply it to martial arts and your day-to-day life. Without allowing it to consume you, occasionally consider how you are feeling, what state your body is in and your general health. With this type of awareness, you will come to understand energy without its formal approach. Take part in energy-related exercises and expose yourself to courses if you feel it is necessary.

The people in the world who show true balance over the life force that I have experienced, of whom there are few, are not typical of martial arts. They have been fortunate to experience changes in their physiology that has led to a clear mental state and view of the world. Often this has not necessarily led to an involvement of martial arts due to the combative aspect upon which all martial art training is based. I think it is important to make this understood in the world of martial arts, especially for people beginning their own journey of self-preservation. It is also important to understand how patient you must be to allow changes to occur.

A common myth in martial arts is having flashes of insight or, as the Japanese say, satori or enlightenment that provides an entirely new outlook on life and wisdom with immediate effect. No one who has ever achieved such a state of mind has claimed such a thing. Records have been written, but only to glorify or make a legend of a romanticised historical figure. I am personally not enlightened; however, I am aware of a shift in perception mentally and certain movement that occurs naturally in training and day-to-day life. This has happened over time. Even those who have had experiences during a moment in their lives have taken years to examine and understand what has actually happened to them. Even monks vigorously practising training regimes to develop Qi must take moments of time to set up their demonstration. This time is not available in a real situation.

You can measure an art on how well it bleeds positivity into your everyday life. This does not mean you should be addicted or consumed, as that is not healthy, but it will be of immense benefit for you/everyone to have something with meaning as a part of your/their life. Martial arts imply bettering oneself. Therefore, I would encourage being inquisitive towards the subject of energy for martial art uses and be open-minded. This is healthy for a human being.

What Is Possible?

I feel the quest of the martial artist is to find out what is possible physically and mentally along with all the facets of the human being. I feel this leads to discovering the root of my being, my human abilities and potential. It has taken a lot of training to realise what the expression of this truly signifies. With this insight, I also ask myself what is physically possible. Therefore, you are without any restrictions or limitations because you ask yourself what is possible for you.

You are free to express yourself in martial arts and work on other areas of your being to increase your totality. The idea of asking yourself this question can be applied to any and every area of your life if you choose. This is important because it's the point of going beyond just carrying out a training exercise each week. For IG, it's not only a class you attend or programme of exercises. Your training goes beyond the weekly regime and becomes a positive part of your life. I began asking myself: How do I strike? How do I survive? Once a level of proficiency is reached and part of the puzzle to that question has been found, you move on to another part or question. You might then ask yourself how to improve your life, your work, relationships, and so forth.

The martial arts, despite some of their raw aggressive nature, has a strong positive drive as you push to improve yourself, which is absorbed by the individual.

If your intent is to find answers, you will find them with this attitude of 'what is possible'. Sometimes, you may not find exactly what you expected at the outset; I haven't on many of my quests. This is because you initially set out with an idea in your mind that requires a different perspective. For example, let's say you want to improve how to read situations better. However, through self-observation you realise that you unintentionally make a nervous gesture that gives away the fact that you are trying to read situations. What started as you wanting to become better at something has now uncovered another path you must journey on to understand why you make these gestures. The key is getting started and asking yourself what is possible for you.

I believe you need something to challenge you in order to grow. What you want and what you need are distinctively different. Please take a moment to ponder on this. Thank you.

Weapons

Any serious martial artist can only benefit immensely from training with weapons and becoming familiar with some of the common arms in today's environment. Traditional arms are excellent as training aids because they can add levels of complexity and thought that is not always present in those of the modern day. For example, the use of a weighted chain or whip is not common today. However, by training with some of these weapons you understand why you have to move in a certain way, such as not hitting yourself and gaining better coordination and control to administer more techniques. In addition, there is the historical stamp on the understanding of humankind's endeavours. Some weapons have changed the course of history and, to a degree, human behaviour. Some traditions have held weapons in great revere in their culture – some tribal and others nations. The sword and the gun are great examples. These two are more obvious, but think how much they have contributed to our history. It is staggering. This subject is vast, and there are times that require special types of training to grasp the full use and resources of what you do. Once again, what is vital in The Way of the Internal Gate is self-exploration and the 'spirit of endurance', which are keys in unveiling the wonderful lessons buried deep within this matter.

In this volume, I will only cover IG's basic premise on the importance of learning and understanding weapons. This is due to its encyclopaedic breadth, which can be both exhilarating and overwhelming.

Maintaining a flexible mind and using our ever-growing awareness, the IG exponent trains to assess in moments the character and versatility of any weapon. Regardless of its shape or mode, whether historic or not and in whatever environment you find yourself in, the base principle is to understand how useful the weapon will be, as well as the consequences of using it.

Once again, it is all related to awareness and experience from your exposure, as we have discussed at length in this volume. These words are important in martial arts, which is why they have great depth and meaning. So, with weaponry, skills learnt are both unique and transferable. Whatever comes to hand, old or new, you cultivate the ability to sense its capabilities and ultimate usefulness in your pursuit of self-preservation.

Concluding this section on martial arts prowess, we have now glimpsed into the foundation and living principles of IG, its application and purpose to enhance your martial arts proficiency. The next and final chapter looks at the control centre of our being, which can make all of the before mentioned a reality: the mind.

CHAPTER 3

Beyond the Physical - Mental Prowess

'It is in the brief moments that exist between interacting with your opponents where the mental training of IG comes into play.'

2nd Gate IG Exponent

The final chapter in this first volume is dedicated to the living principles and considers the mind of the martial artist and its application for martial arts prowess. The skills developed through training incorporates the crucial cultivation and involvement of the world that humankind has created. In the end, it is in the way we attune our minds that makes any kind of genuine adjustments to others and ourselves. As mentioned, the primary purpose of the martial artist is self-preservation and self-realisation. This will bring peace and harmony to oneself, along with the insight and altruistic purpose to share this rare gem with the human race.

The Main Ingredient: The Mind

All the training from the previous chapter, despite making sense, is worth little without the understanding, application and power of the mind. It is the mind that is truly precious. There are countless strategies, movements, tricks and methods. Nevertheless, they all share one thing in common: the mind is master of them all. Without this understanding, your martial art prowess will lack longevity and simply wane in time.

When it comes down to application and the feeling of security in what you can do, the mind is the greatest tool and central to all things. This point cannot be stressed enough. Gaining entrance to the faculties of one's mind and exploring its mastery is the backbone to IG's training methods and entire concept. The one who has cultivated their mind will truly have the advantage if developed with the purest of intentions. Herein lies the greatest clue for the martial artist, regardless of method, and the gargantuan challenge of the human spirit and will.

Despite the advantages of one's body, anyone who has accessed areas of one's mind to fruitful endeavours is the one who has truly trained in the art of self-mastery or at least self-understanding. The comprehension of IG is to start from the mind, allowing the brain to engage in what you are doing, and to become alive in the moment and allow this feeling to open and grow from within you. The intent is required.

Intent: The Deciding Factor

The difference between a good and great martial artist is measured by intent and fortitude. Where the intention is in the reason for doing, the intent is only partially this. With the intent to move, the strength is cultivated along with an awareness of mind and its pureness. Whilst your intent cultivates as an ally, you become stronger in mind and consequently in the body through a forging spirit. This strength can emanate from within, unless you choose to hide it; others can feel its presence as a pressure from that individual. This is a natural capability we all share. So, depending on how pure the feeling, the martial artist or indeed a sensitive enough human being can pick up on this intention. Training through martial arts can help you to hide this intent, but it will become more of a hindrance than a life-saving skill if it disrupts your balance. This privilege alone is that of one's instinct, for honesty in oneself, maintains your balance and steady cultivation in this important facet.

Cultivating intent relies a lot on self-belief, which is why IG epitomises it as a 'living principle'. Intent can be used as a tactic in specific circumstances; knowing when to use it is another skill to learn. Many people train their intention in martial arts for a narrow use, sometimes without any knowledge that it's the intention which is the real skill to cultivate. I refer back to the point about cultivation of the mind and how only genuine change can occur once this has been explored and understood.

Balance

In a natural way, all humans know the feeling of being in or out of balance. It can take time to discover when there is no awareness of this, but eventually we all feel it when we have achieved a degree of equilibrium or when we experience a severe shift of being out of it. We also understand that in the course of nature it is stability that sustains life and preserves it. Terms such as 'unhinged' are simply our expression for saying something or someone is out of balance with themselves. So, we know from a natural perspective that all things need to be brought into balance to experience any kind of true growth. When out of balance, there is a favour in one direction or another; therefore, a potential lack of objectiveness.

Your awareness is the quintessential element, paramount to balancing your whole being on all levels from the physical to the emotional and mental. This balance not only restores your training, but it also plays an integral part in your own security, well-being and happiness. The sheer importance of balance can never be overlooked as it creates the right mental climate for genuine growth. Once you are 'in the zone' mentally, it is far easier to do things and accept what life offers you. Training in balance throughout your entire being is essential to IG. It is recognised early in your martial art voyage that balance is the key piece of the mental jigsaw for your evolution – true growth and real change.

Mental Climate

Whether it is psychosomatic or psychological, learning about how our mind works and improving our own outlook, perception and mental stability are all part of the upgrade of our self. Our mental climate, brought about through training and the balance of one's mind, is a vast area for mental exercises to run deeply into the raw psyche of our humanity and being.

To begin with, there are physical exercises such as balancing, slow and fast movements of techniques and their associated breathing mechanics. Followed by body and mind awareness training, this helps to explore mental stability as the platform for self-understanding and creates clarity of one's mind that points to self-mastery and illumination. Not only does this lead to a relaxed yet poised composition and composure, but the physical excellence of oneself is also lifted, soaring high through the answers and unique potential that you have as an individual on your own path in martial arts. Establishing your mental climate and polishing your mind towards clarity are the seeds for your own ultimate realisation. Now, let us consider some of this raw psyche deeper as well as elements that help us to understand our true being further.

Core Stability: Part 2 – Mind Exploration

In Core Stability: Part 1, the emphasis was on the development of stability and a strong core for your physiology and biology. The same tenet applies to your emotional feelings and expressive aspects of your being, and obviously the mental attributes of one's mind. Although difficult to put into words, core stability in the mind needs to be attempted initially with ideas and exercises that will encourage and help one's being become more stable. A settled mind that leads to becoming a stable person in your totality is the goal. This means exercises that will increase emotional stability and sturdiness. This will lessen things that control you in an excessive manner.

In much of our lives we spend a great deal of time being reactive, responding to things that are around us or coming towards us. This is because the world is such a big, big place and there are so many occurrences and actions that we cannot possibly control. In many cases it can be more difficult to stand out and much easier to go with the flow, such as day in day out as we go to work carrying out a familiar routine and just reacting to what occurs around us. Learning to become mindful and aware of this is your initial step into the next phase of core stability.

Time is the deciding factor in one's life and has the greatest impact. It is a constant continuum and completely out of one's control, but you can make it work to your advantage. It is what we do with our time and what we decide to control that makes a difference. This is what will make a change and help to create a stable mind. People also have different perspectives of time in different life scenarios. Another aspect of time to consider is that it seems to pass quickly when your mind is occupied. Yet, in that same period of time we could be doing something that does not captivate us and time passes more slowly. This demonstrates that you have the capacity to alter your perception and state of mind.

Core stability is to use something whether we have control over it or not, in a positive way. For example, timing is an important issue for the martial artist; each person has a natural rhythm that can be referred to as their timing depending on the circumstance. Without core stability of your own, there's no true way to judge your own timing to then improve it. Some people can do it with ease and judge the timing of others too. It can be quite difficult to do when you think about it.

If you're training in a martial art where you have less control over your opponents from the beginning, then it is much more difficult to control their time or use it to your advantage. You need a lot more precision and pinpoint timing as discussed in previous exercises. Not only do you have to improve your own timing, but also the ability to sense others and what skill they have with timing.

As you continue your martial arts journey, you begin to delve deeper into these thoughts and ideas. At first glance and even for a time they may appear useless to the martial artist, but they will yield interest and reason for exploitation along with self-understanding.

Your own training begins to bear fruit when your perception starts to alter. You find relevance to insights of your being and anthropologically your studies reveal marvels of humanity and your inherent merits. As this self-understanding is realised over time, the more you reap from the realm of martial arts.

As your life and whole being is enhanced and becomes more enjoyable due to achieving core stability of the mind, so we begin with the study and understanding of our emotions. The reason for this is because our emotions are reactive, change rapidly and can cause us to act without reason or thought, which can place us in compromising positions. Dealing with this aspect first gives us greater focus and starts to strengthen the mind prior to the more challenging training of mental exploration ahead. Some people even wonder what emotional training has got to do with martial arts. I would personally say it has everything to do with it. Not only does it channel negative emotions such as anger or self-doubt, but it also helps to be motivated and focused on self-improvement. It also depends on what you want to get out of martial arts and the reasons you study. For me, the mental aspects of martial arts training have created a natural patience with myself, one that is conducive with further learning and self-understanding. Without this, you may find the depths of martial arts eluding you.

IG's training consists of many exercises that are used as a catalyst to find out what affects and concerns you. The exercises require self-examination to gain a deep understanding of yourself. You become aware of your inner voice and the feelings you hold regarding your environments and external factors. This develops a sensitivity, which all who have trained in IG can attest, and with it an awareness that turns inward to gain a greater understanding of the world around them. This is part of the puzzle learnt through IG.

From the outside world, what impacts your personal space and thoughts? Consider this for a moment. Believe me when I tell you that this is essential for your martial arts cultivation and leads to the quest for answers: Who am I? How can I improve? Then you can transfer this knowledge into the ability to read your opponents' actions. IG provides the tools that enable you to find this from within, experience it and channel it for a more productive outcome over time.

So, to recap, the reason for beginning with our emotions is that our brain lacks reason even though it is a sensitive tool that communicates situations and feelings. This lacking trait brings about uncontrollable, undeniable habits or reactions that lead to negative or less favourable events sometimes. Not to mention our own inner thoughts and feelings that can affect our outlook and self-assurance.

Further into your studies of core stability training to deal with your emotional triggers, the balance of your mind and path for mental acuity will deepen and present before you in real time. Progressing further into mental stability is where your mind becomes less troubled, more reasoned and focused. As a martial artist, this is useful to not allow someone or something to stun and distract our mind. It enables us to make decisions with instinct and spontaneity, and trust our inner voice and reason whilst also accepting what happens, knowing that occurrences can happen in or out of favour. It is how we respond and make the best of or channel these that is the most important and beneficial. This is very difficult because things affect us. No matter how stable we are, we can still allow something to get on top of us and certainly make us stumble.

What I have personally found amazing in my training is that I now have a core stability during times when I have been terribly disappointed with myself, or a negative mood has cast over me or something bad has happened, such as being in an accident. It is your perception that changes and offers new opportunities that were once not felt. Even though it sounds strange, a good example is illness. When you are recovering from an illness, your body changes and works differently to heal you. You don't focus solely on the negative feeling or impact, but you become inquisitive and sense strange changes internally. Your overall internal awareness becomes fascinating to watch once you open the door to your internal landscape.

You recognise biological impacts and changes, such as crying and laughter and how they are linked and the benefit they bring to your outlook and improvement as an individual. There is a place that I feel inside of me where I know and understand that this is something I have to go through. It reminds and encourages me to gain something from the experience. Positive or negative, the experience will lead to benefit. So, not only will you grow as an individual in martial arts skills and prowess, your life will grow and you will gain more from it.

Quality of the Mind

The quality of your mind is simply measured by how much time, effort and understanding you put into your training to achieve greater self-knowledge. Also, to an extent, what you are prepared to do to achieve a deeper state of mindfulness. This is the pursuit of the essence where you strive with all you can muster to attain truth and quality, which transforms your perspective to deep meaning versus an accumulative-based knowledge. This will then be applied to your martial art prowess and show in either mental security or superior ability, or it could surface as a negative where the ego wishes to outwit all who cross its path. As described in this volume many times, this is down to the individual, you, and the direction you want to take your training.

The ability to delve deep inside yourself and the opponent with your mind whilst sensing your surroundings will cultivate your awareness. More importantly, you develop the ability to engage with your mind's presence, which unifies your body and mind in concentration. The quality of your mind develops in many layers of your physiology and psyche. In discovering these layers, you will unlock the quality of your mind and essence of your being.

Awareness

This is the key and true beginning to any kind of real improvement. With the ability to keep your mind in the present moment, awareness is like watering a seed that will bloom with continuous sprinkling.

Over time, your awareness will strengthen and you begin to notice smaller happenings you missed before cultivating this ability. The natural following of this force is a kind of mental strength that is capable to sustain poise in your endeavours for longer than your normal capacity. This allows you more effort and time in your self-discovery and enhancement in martial arts prowess. The strength of your awareness will improve and expand. A wider field of your spatial awareness can be cultivated also; naturally, this applies to a grander internal perception too.

To follow is a simple exercise that is common to anyone who studies breathing. This encourages you to develop the presence of mind through awareness.

Awareness with Breathing Exercise:

- ❖ Get into a comfortable position. As a guide, you can sit cross-legged, stand or lie relaxed
- ❖ If possible, but it is not essential, breathe through your nose
- ❖ Close your eyes to enhance your sense of feeling, but again this is not essential
- ❖ Begin to 'watch' your breathing
- ❖ Feel the air entering through your nose and throat
- ❖ Allow your awareness to 'engage' with the pressure that is created by the air, then follow it in and out
- ❖ Begin with a minute of this before building up to five and then ten

This is the beginning, after which this can be taken in a great variety of directions according to your purpose. Simple exercises like this can be underestimated, yet here is where IG excels.

'I find that the breathing exercises in IG energise the body and clear the mind. I'm not sure if I can put the 'why' into words, but after a session of this I feel an increased mass that is balanced with a lighter spirit and faster reaction. This increased the power of punches and kicks and speeded up responses. I guess it helps clear the dross from my mind, allowing me to see more clearly the detail that surrounds me.'

5th Gate IG Exponent

Do It with Feeling!

Without hesitation, you have to apply yourself and work hard even if you don't think you can. All things have a meaning behind them, so we will forever be at their mercy until we train to realise this.

A human being can do anything if the soul is free. If you can't do a move, then that's the first sign. So, why can't you do the move? It could be fear, lack of self-belief, don't believe it is possible, a past conditioning where an emotion restricts physical movement, and so on. This is the individual's free route to the original self. Why do I wish to feel the original self? Because I can sense and feel the restrictions that I have allowed to condition me over time; therefore, I do not feel truly in tune with myself. You could say that right now. I am me but in a conditioned state, yet I feel this is not truly me. This is why feeling in what you do is so important. Sometimes we cannot comprehend something, but there is a good reason for that instinctive feeling – this is imperative to the martial artist.

Don't just do it because you are told to do it. Do it because you want to do it! Feel it, and experience it. You do it as you believe in it. This is martial arts.

Opening the Emotional Gates

Exposure is the essential point here. We have all experienced fear, overexcitement, anger, etc. We need their positive attributes, but how can we diminish the negatives (depending on the interpretation) and foster what's needed from them? Perspective is one way to view and do this. You cannot diminish or change what occurs; however, you can command the way you respond, over time! In other words, we need to channel these emotions and feelings to explore, deepen and open our beings.

These emotions cause tension in our bodies and weaken us, or they can make us more powerful. Pressure is a genuine part of IG and one of the crucial training tools for you to cultivate. By putting ourselves under pressure with balance and awareness to grow, we begin to release more of our natural ability. Great understanding lies in this dangerous realm of martial arts training. This is not stupid danger – we live and grow by the pressure of our attempt to harm ourselves with the perspective of the martial arts, the human being. Exposure is a route journeyed with balance and martial spirit.

The Mind Creates, the Body Expresses

First, you punch in order to make good your strike. Then you think about the position and angle of your arm to make the strike quicker and more damaging. You then feel which parts of the arm movement can be improved and how to do so. Then you think about how to bring your whole body into play to create a livelier punch and also how to deliver not only from a stationary position.

After developing a free-flowing strike, you think of how to add more weight to your strike whilst maintaining speed. Your energy is brought into play through breathing and more methods regarding reactive speed and the central nervous system. Any physical, psychological or emotional blockage that could impede your ability of a punch thrown with self-belief are dealt with. Then, on a mental level, you work with your body. As the mind creates, the body expresses.

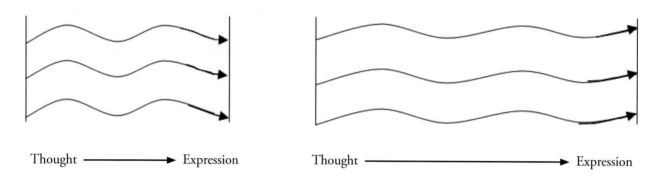

Thought ⟶ Expression   Thought ⟶ Expression

The diagram above illustrates the time it takes for the message of thought in one's mind to become the expression of that idea or thought. The individual on the left is able to express quicker and more effectively than the one on the right. However, this is not to be awed. It is the cultivation of one's training along with the removal of restrictions accumulated through one's life that have become an obstruction to one's natural being.

Here you can understand the terminology 'returning to the natural source of freedom'. I do not say a conditioning is either wholly good or bad, as this requires perception; however, in many cases, they present what can be described as a blockage to one's expression. In the short term, these conditionings may appear important to have because one of the main reasons for their development is to protect oneself and one's beliefs. But, in the long term, remaining 'conditioned' blocks one's full potential. The realisation of this comes from perseverance in self-understanding. At some point, you let go of previous ideas that you have clung to in the past, regardless of their origin. Your awareness and feelings deepen, and you are presented with faith in yourself and what you see through awareness from greater mental acuity. Keep the faith.

Psychologies Part

On a practical and more obvious level, you can imagine how psychology is applied to combat circumstances. The thing about combat, though, is that you won't have much chance or opportunity to play too many psychological games during most attacks. It is easier to see these psychological deficiencies in sports because it is ruled in a certain way to promote justice and fairness. War, combat and the adversary do not have that luxury. Psychology is still used in real combat. It is quick and you have to have your wits about you to be able to cope with it.

So, the obvious things are dampening people's egos, to attack their mind, make them feel weak, make them feel strong and then the opposite, and make them believe something like feigning a strike but following up with a real one. There are many different psychological behaviours and strategies that can be used in combat circumstances and life in general.

Psychology lends itself to a much deeper form of self-realisation. You become more familiar and things are more apparent within a person at this level, but in this case it is more important to study and understand the psychology of yourself. We all have idiosyncrasies along with physical and mental attributes that make up our personality. Looking deeper, we want to understand how psychology plays a part in combat and our own realisations. We can then use it as a tool to enhance self-esteem, ability in combat and how to prevent a situation escalating. It is important that you understand and become aware of these types of strengths and weaknesses in your own self.

So, therefore, psychology plays a part by looking into yourself and starting to deal with your own behaviour. In a way, it is becoming your own psychologist: developing reason, perception and self-understanding. As explained, in martial arts you are your own antithesis. This means you ask how to understand yourself more and use that as a medium.

Like all the living principles in this book, use it to improve your existence, combat an adversary using whatever form it may take, enhance and upgrade your being, and preserve your life. As previously mentioned, in IG we use tools and find exercises that will become a catalyst for discovery in this area of one's mind. We use it to discover one's own psychology and then expand on it by becoming aware of what psychology does, how it can make one stronger or weaker, and what are the real effects of humans.

It is interesting how you become familiar with behaviour and situational understanding. I think any martial artist can understand the real value of this and use it to positively enhance one's life and find peace.

Quality of Life

We are now at the end of the first volume *Living Principles* in this series of *The Way of the Internal Gate*. I believe I have made the message of IG clear. The human spirit and its essence that we all indigenously share is our most precious trait above all things. Our survival will count on the enhancement, support and upgrade of the human being that is balanced and directed by the laws of nature and compassion.

This series is IG's contribution to the world of martial arts in the pursuit of improving one's life. Looking into our immediate and long-term future, these are the elements for genuine survival and self-preservation.

The exponent of IG, through the cultivation and transition of their unique application towards martial arts training, learns to become alive in the moment and acutely aware, to be richer in thought with clarity of mind and expressive in nature. They become happy and poised in spirit and learn with a deep understanding of their internal landscape, which is in tune with the outside world through one's self-knowledge to increase quality of life. The mission of IG is to raise and upgrade the human being, seeing this as the way to preserving life and, indeed, the human species.

Thank you for reading this book and giving your time to learn about The Way of the Internal Gate.

Experience

I sincerely hope that you've been able to experience something of IG and it has been of value to you in some way whilst reading through these pages. IG's goal is to truly help the human being and add quality to your life. I hope this book has inspired, guided and planted seeds for you to harvest.

Whatever training you do and wherever you are, whether you train in martial arts or have never done so in your life, I would like you to know that myself and the IG exponents are always ready to listen and train with you and anyone wishing to embark on their martial arts journey. I believe without hesitation that The Way of the Internal Gate has an altruistic purpose for humanity which can benefit all.

To experience and enhance is the ultimate goal, regardless of the origin. With that, I would be happy to hear from you whether you train in IG or not. If you have adopted some of the philosophy or ideas presented in this book, then I will have succeeded in being helpful to my fellow human being.

About the Author

Ade Finch is the founder of The Way of the Internal Gate Martial Art, which has been created to empower the individual to unearth and recognise their own martial arts voyage and journey of self-discovery. By using IG as a vehicle to reach the root and essence of martial arts, it will help to catapult the skill of the individual.

Ade has trained in martial arts for over 30 years and enjoys sharing his knowledge and experience with like-minded souls who are open to exposing themselves in the pursuit of martial arts prowess and self-understanding.

The Way of the Internal Gate is based in North Derbyshire, UK, and offers training around the world with retreats, seminars and private tuition. Mr Finch guides you through self-understanding, awareness, applications for self-preservation, weaponry and many related subjects to uncover your spirit of forbearance required to discover your true self.

Printed in the United States
By Bookmasters